Drew Provan

iPhone

in easy steps

Covers iPhone 4

In Easy Steps is an imprint of In Easy Steps Limited
Southfield Road · Southam
Warwickshire CV47 0FB · United Kingdom
www.ineasysteps.com

Second Edition

Notice of Liability
Every effort has been made to ensure that this book contains accurate
and current information. However, In Easy Steps Limited and the
author shall not be liable for any loss or damage suffered by readers
as a result of any information contained herein.

Trademarks
All trademarks are acknowledged as belonging to their respective
companies.

In Easy Steps Limited supports The Forest Stewardship Council (FSC),
the leading international forest certification organisation. All our titles
that are printed on Greenpeace approved FSC certified paper carry the
FSC logo.

MIX
Paper from
responsible sources
FSC www.fsc.org   FSC® C020837

Printed and bound in the United Kingdom

ISBN 978-1-84078-415-2

Contents

7   Accessing the Internet   155

11 Solving Problems 221

Index 233

1 The iPhone

The iPhone is a sophisticated and highly capable cell phone which is able to make calls, send text and multimedia messages, browse the web, keep contacts and calendars synchronized with desktop Macs or PCs, take and store video images and still photos, play games and keep you organized professionally and personally.

What Exactly is the iPhone?

Why has there been so much hype surrounding the iPhone? Cellular phones have been around for years. Many of them can play music, movies, browse the web and function as personal digital assistants (PDAs). So what's so special about the Apple iPhone?

Apple's first generation iPhone was launched in June 2007. Because of the advance publicity there was a feeding frenzy when launch day came, with customers queuing for many hours to get their hands on an iPhone.

There are several reasons for the excitement, including the Apple brand (stylish, functional and innovative), people already loved the iPod so a cell phone with iPod capabilities and a widescreen had major appeal. The sheer simplicity of operation, using a touch screen rather than a plethora of buttons, had major appeal.

So this was a cell phone unlike any other. In addition to the usual telephony capabilities, this phone could play music, videos, YouTube and more. It could be used as a diary with easy synchronization to Microsoft Outlook or Apple iCal. It would handle email (including Exchange Server) more easily. Its SMS program made messaging a breeze. Its browser made browsing the web easier than previous smartphones.

In addition, there were other applications such as Weather, Stocks, Maps and others. Despite criticisms from some quarters regarding the poor camera (2 megapixels in the first and second generation iPhones) and lack of video, along with the inability for the user to add more applications, the first generation iPhone was a huge success.

The second generation iPhone was launched in July 2008 and brought with it 3G, a much faster data network connection. In June 2009 the 3GS ("S" stands for "speed") was launched. The new iPhone 3GS brought with it the ability to capture video, Voice Control, which enables users to control the iPhone 3GS using voice commands, and numerous other features.

The 4G iPhone was launched in June 2010 and brought with it many refinements such as dual cameras, camera flash, FaceTime, higher resolution Retina Display screen and many other improvements over the previous models.

What Does It Do?

It would be easier to ask what it *doesn't* do! The iPhone, even as a basic cell phone, before you start adding applications, has many functions — probably enough for most people, without actually having to add more apps of your own. But, since there are *thousands* of applications available for download, you can extend the functionality of the iPhone way beyond this. The iPhone is more like a small computer since you can store files, connect to other desktop computers, view documents including Word and PDF files, play games, look up recipes, manage your time, and many other functions.

Hot tip

The iPhone is more like a computer than a standard cell phone.

Work

Make phone calls
Manage your diary
Check email
Check Visual Voicemail
Maintain your contacts list
Check stocks and shares
Take Voice Memos
Takes notes using Notepad
Do the math with Calculator

Expand your iPhone

Buy music, films and audiobooks
Customize your iPhone 3GS
Buy apps or download free apps
Store files
Open Word and other docs
Connect to desktop Mac or PC
Turn iPhone into a remote control
Find recipes
Play games

Play

Send SMS or MMS
Chat using Skype and other apps
Look at photos and videos
Watch YouTube
Never get lost again! Use Maps and GPS
See weather in multiple locations
Clock, alarm and stop-watch
Calculator
Listen to music or watch videos
Browse the web

iPhone 4G Specifications

Cellular and wireless capabilities

The iPhone 4G is a Quad band phone which uses GSM and GPRS/EDGE.

There is also built-in Wi-Fi (802.11b/g) and Bluetooth. The iPhone also includes Global Positioning System (GPS) software, making is easy to geotag your pictures and videos.

Battery

Unlike most cell phones, the user cannot take the battery out for replacement. The iPhone uses a built-in battery which is charged using a USB connection to the computer, or using the charger supplied by Apple.

What do you get from a full charge?

Activity	Hours
Talk time	7 (3G)
Standby	300
Internet use	10 (Wi-Fi) 6 (3G)
Video playback	10
Audio playback	40

Internal storage

The iPhone uses internal flash drive storage. There is no SD or other card slot so the internal flash memory is all the storage you have — use it wisely!

The iPhone 4G is available with 16GB or 32GB storage capacity, whereas the older iPhone 3GS is only available with 8GB.

If you intend to keep a number of videos as well as music on your iPhone it may be wise to opt for the higher capacity iPhone. In terms of color, you can get the iPhone in black or white.

Beware

You cannot remove the iPhone battery. This has to be carried out by Apple.

What can I do with the storage space?

	8GB	16GB	32GB
Songs	1,750	3,500	7,000
Videos	10 hours	20 hours	40 hours
Photos	10,000	20,000	25,000

Sensors in the iPhone

There are 4 sensors in the iPhone 4G: the Three-Axis Gyro, the Accelerometer, Proximity Sensor and the Ambient Light Sensor.

The *Accelerometer* enables the phone to detect rotation and position. This is important when switching from portrait to landscape viewing. The Accelerometer is also used in many of the iPhone game apps such as *Labyrinth* (below) which uses the accelerometer to good effect — as you tilt the iPhone the ball bearing moves across a virtual board.

The *Proximity Sensor* switches off the iPhone screen when you make a call — it senses that the phone is close to the ear, saving valuable power. The *Ambient Light Sensor* adjusts the iPhone screen to the ambient lighting, again saving energy if a bright screen is not required.

The iPhone Itself

Unlike most cell phones, the iPhone is unusual since it has very few physical buttons.

Buttons you need to know on the iPhone

- Sleep & wake (On/Off)
- Ring/silent
- Volume controls
- Home button

Hot tip

Press the Sleep/Wake (On/Off) button as soon as you have finished using the iPhone — this helps conserve battery power.

14

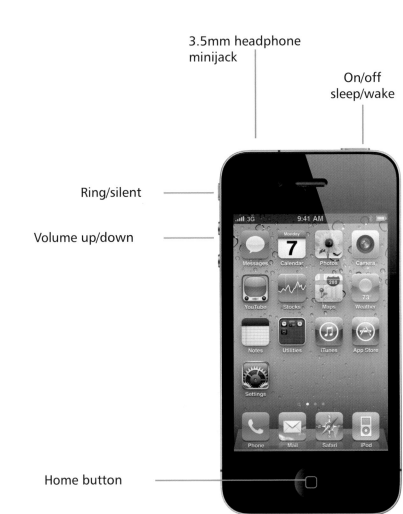

3.5mm headphone minijack

On/off sleep/wake

Ring/silent

Volume up/down

Home button

Sleep/wake

Press and briefly hold this button if your iPhone is switched off. You will see the Apple logo and the loading screen will start up. You will then be taken to the Home screen (opposite page). If you wish to put your phone away, press the Sleep/Wake button to put your phone to sleep. This button is also useful if you wish to forward a caller to Voicemail.

Ring/silent

You often want your phone on silent, during meetings for example. The Ring/Silent button can be toggled up and down. When you see the red dot, this means the iPhone is on silent.

Ring/silent

This position is Sounds ON
Flip down for Sounds OFF

The Home button

This does what the name suggests and brings you back to the Home page from wherever you are. If you are browsing applications in another screen, pressing the Home button will bring you right back to the Home page. If you are using an app, pressing Home will close the app. If you are on a phone call, pressing the Home button lets you access your email or other apps.

Hot tip

Pressing the The Home button quits an app, and if you press again it will take you back to the Home Screen.

Press here to return to the Home screen or quit an application

Other Buttons on the iPhone

Volume controls

This is a rocker button. Pressing the upper half will increase the volume and the lower half will reduce the volume. You can easily adjust the volume of the audio output when you are listening to the iPod, YouTube, or when you are making a phone call. If you cannot hear the caller very well try increasing the volume.

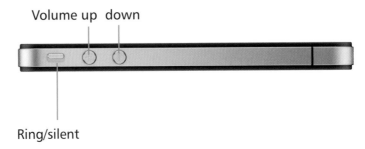

Volume up down

Ring/silent

The Micro SIM slot

The iPhone 4G uses a Micro SIM (much smaller than standard SIM which is used older iPhone models). Apple provides a SIM removal tool in the iPhone box. You will find it attached to the small white pack, on the inner cover.

Insert SIM tool into this hole and push down. The SIM card holder will pop up and you can remove or insert a SIM card

Dock connector, speaker and microphone

These are located at the bottom of the iPhone.

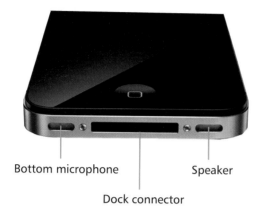

Bottom microphone   Speaker

Dock connector

Back view of the iPhone 4G

This shows the location of the main camera and the LED flash (flash is not available for the front camera).

Main camera ⎯⎯⎯⎯⎯

LED Flash ⎯⎯⎯⎯⎯

The Home Screen

What's on the Home Screen?

When you turn the iPhone on you will see some icons which are fixed, such as the top bar with the time and battery charge indicator, as well as the dock at the bottom which holds 4 apps. By default, your iPhone will have Phone, Mail, Safari and iPod on the bottom dock. You can move these off the dock if you want, but Apple puts these here because they are the most commonly used apps, and having them on the dock makes them easy to find.

Just above the dock you will see a magnifying glass and two or more dots. The dots represent each of your screens — the more apps you install, the more screens you will need to accommodate them (you are allowed 11 in all). The illustration here shows an iPhone with two screens, and the Home Screen is the one we are viewing. If you flicked to the next screen, the second dot would be white and the first one would be black. In effect, these are meant to let you know where you are at any time.

Beware

The Battery indicator is fairly crude. For a more accurate guide, try switching on Battery %.

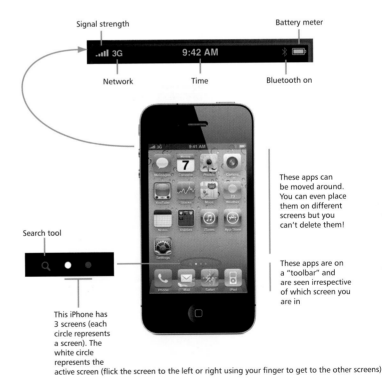

Signal strength

Battery meter

.ıll 3G   9:42 AM   Bluetooth on

Network   Time

These apps can be moved around. You can even place them on different screens but you can't delete them!

Search tool

These apps are on a "toolbar" and are seen irrespective of which screen you are in

This iPhone has 3 screens (each circle represents a screen). The white circle represents the active screen (flick the screen to the left or right using your finger to get to the other screens)

Default Applications

The iPhone comes with applications that are part of the operating system. The core set here cannot be deleted.

 For sending SMS and MMS messages

 Notepad

 Don't forget

You cannot delete any of the standard apps — only the ones you add yourself.

 Calendar app. This icon is dynamic (*the date changes*)

 Clock, alarm and stopwatch app

 Camera and synced photos are stored here

 Calculator

 Stills or movie camera

 System and app settings are stored here

 YouTube video app

 iTunes music store

 Stocks and Shares

 The Apple App Store where you can get free or paid apps

 Maps and GPS system

 Use this icon when you want to make a phone call

 Weather app

 Email app

 Voice Memos app

 Safari Internet browser

 Game Center

 iPod for music, audiobooks, podcasts, and movies

19

Software version iOS4.2

Apple's update of the iPhone software from 3 to 4, and more specifically, to 4.2 has brought several improvements, including:

Multitasking

The iPhone can now run several applications at the one time. All running apps can be seen in the App Tray (or "multitasking bar" — the real name is not quite clear!).

Folders

Apps can now be placed in folders, freeing up space on the Home Screens.

AirPrint

The iPhone and iPad can now print wirelessly (although currently only to a handful of Hewlett-Packard printers. You can print to many printers using 3rd-party apps such as Printopia (*http://ecamm.com/mac/printopia/*).

AirPlay

The iPhone can be used to stream content to Apple TV (2nd generation only) or AirPort Express.

Landscape keyboard for Mail, Messages, Notes and Safari

All the Apple apps work in landscape mode, and many third party apps use this feature too. In landscape, the keyboard is wider, the keys are larger and it is easier to type accurately when replying to emails or sending SMS or MMS messages.

Voice Memos

As the name suggests, this allows you to record voice notes.

Improved Calendar application
The Calendar app now communicates with Microsoft Exchange ActiveSync.

Internet Tethering
Allows sharing of the iPhone's Internet connection with a laptop.

Parental controls

New languages
The iPhone supports 30 languages and 40 keyboards.

MobileMe, Find My Phone and Remote Wipe
Find My Phone was previously available only to MobileMe subscribers, but with iOS4.2 it has become free for anyone wishing to use it.

Spotlight searching
Apple's OS X uses Spotlight to index and find files. This search facility is now available on the iPhone, making it easy to find appointments, notes, contacts or text within emails.

Hot tip

Spotlight searching works like a dream on the iPhone — use it if you want to find appointments, contacts and other items.

21

Other features
Include automatic Wi-Fi login and YouTube login.

The Touch Screen Display

The iPhone uses a touch-sensitive screen for input, using gestures and a virtual keyboard. The screen is 3.5 inches or 88.9 mms (diagonal) and has a resolution of 960 x 640 pixels, giving a resolution of 326 ppi — Apple has called this the *Retina Display* because the resolution is so high. This results in great clarity when viewing the browser or watching movies on the iPhone. Although the iPhone has a fingerprint-resistant coating it still gets grubby. A number of companies make screen protectors (sticky plastic sheets that cover the entire screen) but they are probably not necessary since the screen is made from scratch-resistant glass. You can also protect the other parts of the iPhone from scratching by using a protective case.

Touch screen features

The screen is able to detect touch using skin. If you wear gloves or try to tap the screen using a stylus nothing will happen — it responds best to skin.

Tapping

Tapping with one finger is used for lots of apps. It's a bit like clicking with the mouse. You tap apps to open them, to open hyperlinks, to select photo albums which then open, to enter text using the keyboard, and many other tasks.

Sliding

Sliding is another common action. When you first press the iPhone Home button you will see an option at the bottom of the screen to Slide to Unlock. Putting your finger on the arrow button then sliding all the way to the right will then take you to the Home Screen. You also use the slide action to answer phone calls and shut down the iPhone.

Dragging

This is used to move documents that occupy more than a screen's worth across the screen. Maps use this feature, as do web pages. Place your finger on the screen, keep it there and move the image below to where you want it.

Pinching and spreading

If you are looking at a photo or text which you want to enlarge, you can spread two fingers apart and the image will become larger. Keep doing this till it's the size you want. If you want to zoom out and make the image smaller, pinch your fingers together.

Beware

The touch screen will only work with skin, so don't bother trying to use a stylus, your nails or wearing gloves. It won't work!

Flicking

If you are faced with a long list, e.g. in Contacts, you can flick the list up or down by placing your finger at the bottom or top of the screen, keep your finger on the screen, then flick your finger downwards or upwards and the list will fly up or down.

Shake the iPhone

When entering text or copying and pasting, to undo what you have done, shake the iPhone. Shake again to redo.

Portrait or landscape mode

The iPhone is generally viewed in a portrait mode but for many tasks it is easier to turn the iPhone and work in landscape mode. If you're in Mail, or using Safari, the text will be larger. More importantly, the keys of the virtual keyboard will become larger making it easier to type accurately.

Entering text

The iPhone has predictive text, but this is unlike any you may have used before. The accuracy is astonishing. As you type, the iPhone will make suggestions before you complete a word. If you agree with the suggested word, tap the spacebar. If you disagree, tap the small "x" next to the word.

Hot tip

You can shake your iPhone to skip audio tracks, undo and redo text, and more.

Hot tip

To accept a spelling suggestion tap the spacebar. Reject the suggestion by clicking the "x". Over time your iPhone will learn new words.

Hot tip

Tapping the spacebar with two fingers at the same time also inserts a period.

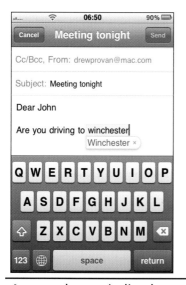

Accept the capitalized word by tapping the spacebar

Accept the apostrophe by tapping the spacebar

The Virtual Keyboard

Hot tip

The iPhone has done away with virtually all buttons and provides a software-based QWERTY keyboard. The keyboard becomes visible automatically when needed.

The keys are small but when you touch them they become larger, which increases accuracy. The letter "L" below has been pressed and has become much larger.

There are all the usual features of a computer keyboard, including spacebar, delete key ⌫, shift ⇧, numbers and symbols .?123

To correct a word, touch the word you want to correct and hold your finger on the word. You will see a magnifying glass. Move your finger to where you want the insertion point (|) to be, stop there and delete any wrong letters

The keyboard has automatic spellcheck and correction of misspelled words. It has a dynamic dictionary (learns new words). Some keys have multiple options if you hold them down, e.g. hold down the £ key and you see:

Hot tip

Some keys such as Currency and URL endings can be accessed by holding down the key. A pop-up will show the options.

Where's Caps Lock?

It is frustrating hitting the CAPS key for every letter if you want to type a complete word in upper case. But you can activate Caps Lock easily:

- Go to **Settings**

- Select **Keyboard**

- Make sure the **Caps Lock** slider is set to **ON**

- While you are there, make sure the other settings are on, for example "." **Shortcut** — this helps you add a period by tapping the spacebar twice (much like the BlackBerry)

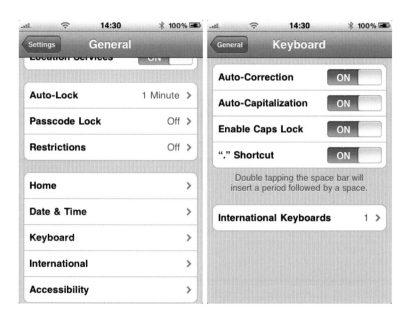

Other settings for the keyboard

- **Autocorrection** suggests the correct word. If it annoys you, switch it off

- **Autocapitalization** is great for putting capitals in names

- The **"." Shortcut** types a period every time you hit the spacebar twice. This saves time when typing long emails but if you prefer not to use this, switch it off. Here's another neat trick — you can also insert a period by tapping the spacebar with 2 fingers simultaneously

Beware

Unlike conventional cell phones, you have to register your iPhone with Apple before you can use it.

Register Your iPhone

Before you can do anything on your iPhone you will need to register with your phone provider. Unlike other cell phones, this is done via iTunes. You will need to have the latest version of iTunes running on your PC or Mac. Plug the iPhone into your computer and iTunes should open automatically. You should then see:

Click **Continue** and agree to the License Agreement.

You will be prompted for your Apple ID. If you don't have one you will need to set one up. Apple makes this pretty painless and leads you through the whole process.

Don't forget

You need to set yourself up with an Apple ID. Do this using iTunes.

What you see next will depend on whether you are registering your first iPhone or upgrading from a previous iPhone. Here we are upgrading:

Follow the prompts and register your new iPhone. Once everything is set up you will not need to do this again, unless you replace your handset or upgrade your iPhone.

Synchronize Data with a PC

You can choose exactly what you want to sync each time you plug the iPhone into the computer. You will most likely have more music, video and photos than can fit onto the iPhone, even if you have the highest capacity iPhone.

Syncing is easy, but setting up depends on whether you are using a PC or a Mac.

Syncing data using a PC

Use the iPhone Configuration Utility (free download) to sync email, contacts, calendar information and other data. Click the tabs in the left hand column and set up each of these in turn. You can fine tune the settings in iTunes, for example you can choose which photo and music libraries to sync.

You can tell the computer exactly what to sync using iTunes.

Automatic syncing of data using MobileMe

MobileMe requires an annual subscription and it allows you to sync all your data automatically via the "cloud". Essentially, you add appointments or contacts using your PC or Mac and these are sent to the cloud. The data is then sent to your Mac or PC

Hot tip

MobileMe lets you sync emails, contacts, calendars and other items wirelessly (no need to physically plug the iPhone into the computer).

so that your calendars, contacts and other data are identical. Any data added to your iPhone will be sent to your Mac or PC.

You will need to sign up for an account and pay the annual fee.

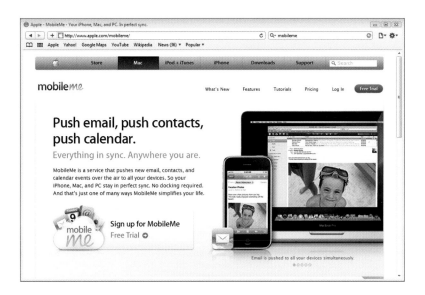

Both Mac and PC have Control Panels which allow you to determine what information is synced and how often the syncing takes place.

This shows the Windows MobileMe Control Panel. After checking the Sync with MobileMe box, you can check Contacts, Calendars and Bookmarks depending on what you want to sync. You can also let MobileMe sync your data automatically.

Synchronize Data with a Mac

Syncing data with the Mac is very straightforward

- Plug the iPhone into the Mac

- iTunes will open automatically

- Click on the iPhone icon on the left of the iTunes window

- Work your way through the tabs selecting what to sync

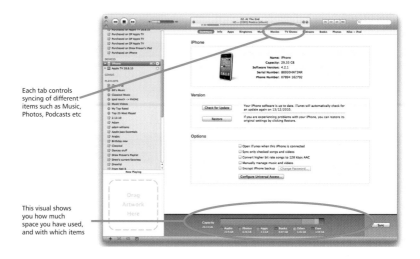

Each tab controls syncing of different items such as Music, Photos, Podcasts etc

This visual shows you how much space you have used, and with which items

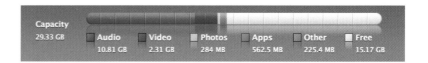

Capacity	Audio	Video	Photos	Apps	Other	Free
29.33 GB	10.81 GB	2.31 GB	284 MB	562.5 MB	225.4 MB	15.17 GB

How much space do I have left?

The picture above shows an iPhone plugged into the Mac. At the bottom of the iTunes window you can see a bar representing the total iPhone capacity. This one has about 15GB free.

Be selective in the items you sync

The largest item on the iPhone is music, which takes up almost 11GB. Each type of sync item (Music, Video, Photos, etc.) is given a different color, so you can see at a glance what's taking up the space. If you are running out of room because you have too many videos on the iPhone, you can go to the Video tab and deselect one or more videos then hit Apply. Those files will then be removed from the iPhone.

Uncheck videos
then hit Apply
to remove them
from the iPhone 3GS

What can be synced?

- Contacts

- Calendars

- Email accounts

- Web page bookmarks

- Notes

- Ringtones

- Music and audiobooks

- Photos

- Podcasts

- Movies

- TV shows

- Music videos

- Applications from the app store

Backup and Restore

Each time you plug the iPhone into your computer it will backup your data, then it will synchronize your iPhone using the settings on your computer. If you have added new photos or music these will be sent to the iPhone.

If you look at the top of the iTunes window when you connect the phone you will see the iPhone being backed up, then synced.

This is what you see at the top of the iTunes window during the synchronization process:

Hot tip

Plug your iPhone into your PC or Mac regularly. This ensures you have a recent backup file in the event your iPhone needs to be restored.

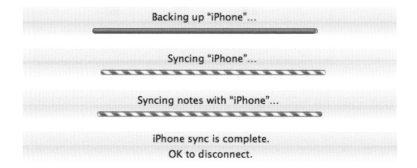

Normally things work well but occasionally the iPhone, like any electronic device, can misbehave. Just as you might restore Windows from a snapshot, so too can you restore the iPhone back to the last working version. If you are syncing your iPhone on a regular basis, you will have a recent backup from which to restore. If you have not been syncing and creating backups, you may have to erase the iPhone and reconfigure.

Hot tip

Unlike an iPod, where you have to eject an iPod from the PC or Mac before unplugging, you don't have to eject the iPhone — simply unplug it.

To restore the iPhone from a backup

Click on the iPhone icon in the iTunes window. This will take you to the iTunes window which will give you the restore option.

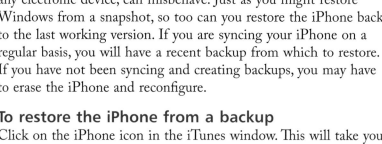

Click here to get to the Restore window

Click **Restore**:

Are you sure you want to restore the iPhone "iPhone" to its factory settings? All of your media and other data will be erased.

iTunes will verify the restore with Apple. After this process is complete, you will have the option to restore your contacts, calendars, text messages and other settings.

Cancel   Restore

Once you click **Restore** you will be led through the whole process, during which the iPhone will be erased and the latest saved iPhone state will be restored. Your iPhone should then function as normal.

It's a good idea to sync your iPhone with iTunes fairly often even if you do not sync music, video or apps. You can plug the iPhone into a wall charger, but you lack the backup files needed for a restore should your iPhone become unstable and need to be restored from a previous snapshot.

Airplane Mode

When to use this mode

There are times when using the cellular or data networks is not allowed, for example when on an aircraft. Some cell phones allow you to switch off GPRS, EDGE, Wi-Fi, and Bluetooth individually before take-off. The iPhone has a single Airplane mode setting that switches off all these communications, making it safe for you to use your iPhone to watch movies or listen to music on the flight.

Airplane mode is also very useful if you want to conserve battery power, since using the cellular network, Wi-Fi and Bluetooth drains the power on the iPhone. If you don't need these, switch them off.

Where is it?

Go to **Settings** and slide the button beside **Airplane Mode** to the right.

How do you know Airplane Mode is switched on?

You can tell by the icon on the top left of the iPhone. You will see a picture of an airplane:

You should see symbol of a plane here when Airplane Mode is on

The other icons to look for include the cellular network icon, Wi-Fi and Bluetooth. It is very obvious when these are on.

Cellular network **ON**   Wi-Fi **ON**   Bluetooth **ON**

Headphones

Apple supplies headphones that look a bit like iPod headphones. But there is a major difference, the iPhone headphones have a control on the right earpiece cable. This control houses the microphone needed for phone conversations when the headphones are plugged in. The control also allows the audio volume to be adjusted to make it louder or quieter.

By clicking the control, audio will pause. Two clicks in quick succession will skip to the next track.

Hot tip

The iPhone headphones are highly sophisticated and can be used to make calls, and divert callers to voicemail.

Press here ONCE to pause audio or answer call (press again at end of call)

To decline call press and hold for ~2 seconds

To switch to incoming or on-hold call, press once

Press here TWICE to skip to next track

To use Voice Control, press and hold

(this tiny control unit also contains the microphone!)

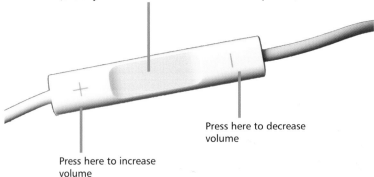

Press here to decrease volume

Press here to increase volume

Uses for the headphones — this is pretty obvious but consider:

- Listening to music, podcasts, audio books
- Listening to the radio
- Watching movies
- Making phone calls
- Dictating VoiceMemos
- Giving Voice commands to your iPhone

Audio and Video Playback

As you would expect, the iPhone supports a number of audio and video formats. The iPhone supports audio in the form of AAC, Protected AAC, MP3, MP3 VBF, Audible (formats 2, 3, and 4), Apple Lossless, AIFF and WAV. In terms of video, the iPhone supports video at 640 x 480 pixels, 30 frames per second (fps), .m4v, .mp4, .mov and MPEG-4 files.

Audio files are played using the iPod app in portrait or landscape mode. Video content, including YouTube, is played only in landscape mode as shown above.

Camera

The iPhone 4G has a main camera (back of phone) and a second camera on the front. The main camera is 5 megapixels, and can shoot high resolution stills and HD video. The main camera also has a flash. The front VGA camera is used for FaceTime calls, and can takes photos and videos of you. The main camera has Tap-to-Focus and a macro autofocus (~10cm).

Both photos and videos can be geotagged, so you can see where in the world you were when the photo or video was shot.

Hot tip

You can take better night pictures if you use the Night Camera app.

Hot tip

Geotagging helps you determine where the photo was taken but you need to switch on Settings > Location Services.

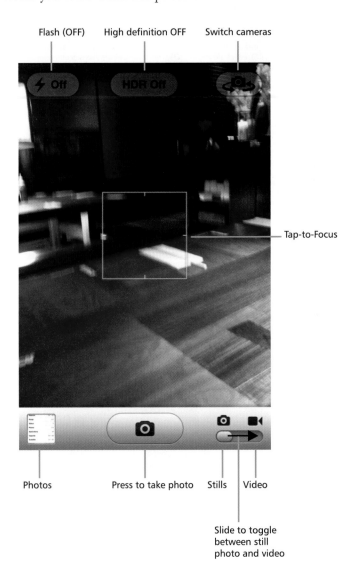

Flash (OFF) High definition OFF Switch cameras

Tap-to-Focus

Photos Press to take photo Stills Video

Slide to toggle between still photo and video

Shooting video

Slide the Stills/Video control to the right and you will see a
Record button (red circle). Click to record video then click again
to stop. The video will be stored and transferred to the computer
when you next sync. Alternatively, you can email or MMS the
video.

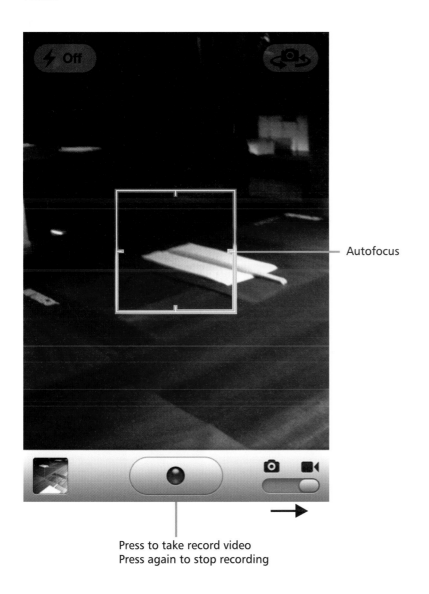

Autofocus

Press to take record video
Press again to stop recording

Customizing the iPhone

Applications

The iPhone comes with many apps preinstalled by Apple. These can be moved around, or even placed on a different screen, but you cannot delete them from the iPhone. These apps are the core features of the iPhone.

The App Store has thousands of apps which we will look at later. Many are free while others are available for purchase. With so many apps available for download the chances are that there will be an app for most things you might want to do.

Ringtones

Apple has supplied several but people will always want to have their own unique ringtone. You can buy these from the App Store or make your own using iTunes or GarageBand. You can assign a specific ringtone to someone in your Contacts list so you know it's them calling when the phone rings.

Backgrounds and wallpapers

Again, there are several to choose from but you can make your own (use one of your photos) or you can download from third party suppliers. Try browsing the Internet for wallpapers or use a specific app.

Accessorizing the iPhone

You can use a screen protector to prevent scratches on the screen. There are many iPhone cases available. These are mainly plastic but leather cases are available as well. Placing your iPhone in a case or cover helps prevent marks or scratches on the phone.

Headphones

If you want to use headphones other than those provided by Apple, that's fine. You may get better sound from your music but you will not have the inbuilt microphone, which is very useful when you make a phone call.

Bluetooth earpieces

Apple has designed a Bluetooth earpiece specifically for the iPhone. This is shown below. Other manufacturers make Bluetooth headsets and earpieces which will work equally well.

Beware

Bluetooth drains power on your iPhone. Try to switch it off if you don't need it.

iPhone docks and cradles

There are many to choose from. These charge your iPhone and many let you listen to music through speakers.

User Settings

There are many settings you can adjust in order to set the iPhone up to work the way you want. These will be discussed in detail later but they are shown briefly here.

As well as the settings already on the iPhone, many apps will have panels for their settings. If an app is not working the way you want, have a look under the Settings Control Panel and scroll to the bottom to see if your app has installed a settings panel.

Wi-Fi
Keep this off if you want to conserve power. Switching it on will let you join wireless networks, if they are open or if you have the password.

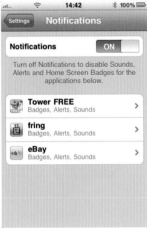

Notifications
You can allow applications, such as Skype and others, to notify you of messages even if the program is not running. This means that if you are using an app like Skype, but you are using another app when a friend sends you a message, a notification will appear on your screen to let you know you have received a message.

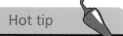
Sounds

You can place the phone on vibrate or have the ringtone on. You can assign different tones for different contacts.

Brightness

The iPhone will adjust brightness automatically. If you always prefer it dimmer or brighter — switch automatic brightness off.

Wallpaper

Wallpaper is what you see when you press the Home Button when the iPhone is locked. Use you own images or download from third party suppliers.

The image above shows a third party wallpaper from the app *Backgrounds*. You can download as many wallpapers as you like and change them whenever you want.

43

Passcode Lock

If you want to prevent people using your phone, add a passcode lock. This is a 4-digit password which will keep the iPhone contents free from prying eyes. You can also choose a complex passcode.

For added security you can switch on the *Wipe After 10 Failed Attempts* setting to prevent data theft.

International

Here you can choose the language and keyboard you wish to use.

You can activate multiple International languages if you use more than one. Activating the Korean keyboard is very useful if you want to change the font in the Notes app (*see* Chapter 6).

Accessibility

For people who have difficulties with vision or sound, there are many tools on the iPhone that can help the user obtain full functionality from their iPhone.

These features are described in greater detail in Chapter 9.

Reset

If all else fails, and your iPhone is causing problems, reset it back to factory conditions.

This is covered in greater detail in Chapter 11.

Here are the settings (preferences) for some of the apps installed on this iPhone. Not every app will install a settings panel but many do. It's worth checking Settings after you install an app to see if it has installed a settings file, since it may contain useful features to help you set it up exactly the way you want.

There are also settings options for:
Bluetooth

Keep this switched off when not needed (Bluetooth and Wi-Fi will drain your power faster). If you want to connect a Bluetooth headset or earpiece you will need to switch Bluetooth on and pair with your device.

Home Screen

You can go with the default Home Screen or choose your own.

Date and Time

This Control Panel adjusts the Date and Time.

Data Roaming

Most of us travel abroad for business or pleasure. We like to take our cell phones to keep in touch with friends, family and the office. Call charges are much higher from overseas, and if you want to receive data (email, browse the web, and other activities) you will need to switch on Data Roaming.

Switch on Data Roaming

Beware

Data Roaming allows you to receive data when away from your home country, but is very expensive.

1 Go to **Settings** > **General** > **Network**

2 Switch **Data Roaming** ON if required

3 Switch OFF when not needed

But beware — the cost of receiving data is very high and will be added to your phone bill. Your data package with AT&T, or other operators, does not cover the cost of downloading data using foreign networks!

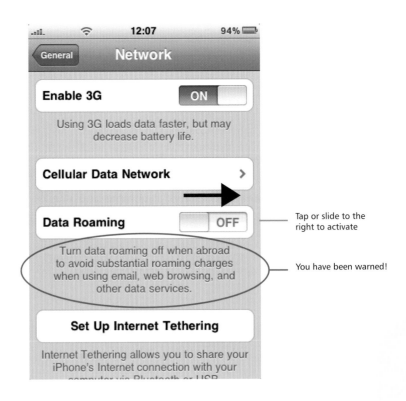

Tap or slide to the right to activate

You have been warned!

46

2 The Phone Functions

In this section we will look at how to use the phone functions, maintain contact lists, make calls using FaceTime, and keep these in sync with desktop computers. The chapter also explores Visual Voicemail, a revolutionary way to see your voicemail messages.

Assigning Ringtones

The iPhone has a number of polyphonic ringtones built in, or you can buy more from iTunes or even make your own. You can have the default tone for every caller or you can assign a specific tone for a contact.

To assign a ringtone:

1 Select contact

2 Under **Ringtone** press the right arrow

3 Choose the ringtone you wish to assign

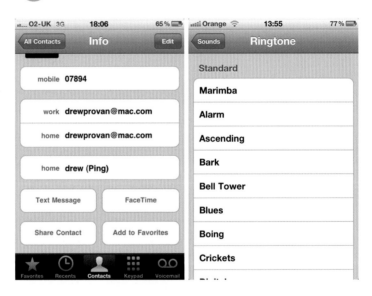

Hot tip

If you use a Mac, GarageBand is a great tool for creating custom ringtones. For instructions on using GarageBand to make ringtones see http://support.apple.com/kb/HT1358.

Obtaining new ringtones

You can buy these from the app store or make your own using GarageBand (Mac) or iTunes.

Making Calls Using Keypad

Select the keypad icon. This brings up a standard keypad on the touch screen. Dial the number.

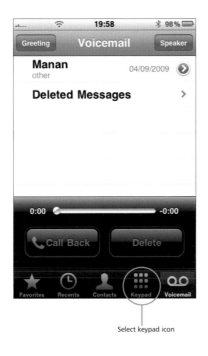

Select keypad icon

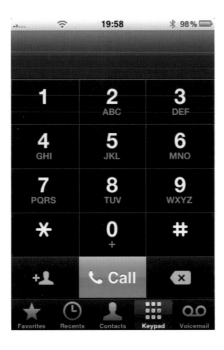

Make FaceTime Video Calls

Video calling became possible with the introduction of a second, front-facing, camera in the iPhone 4G.

To use FaceTime

- The caller and recipient must both use iPhone 4G

- Alternatively, you can use a Mac, running the FaceTime beta (*http://www.apple.com/uk/mac/facetime/?sissr=1*. The PC version had not been released at time of going to press)

- Both caller and recipient must be using Wi-Fi (not 3G)

The FaceTime settings

1 Go to **Settings > Phone > FaceTime > ON**

2 Select contact you wish to call

3 Tap **FaceTime**

4 Make FaceTime call

5 Recipient must tap **Accept**

If you have already had a FaceTime video call with someone you can go to Recents and make another FaceTime call.

Actions during a FaceTime call

Mute the call	Tap ICON. You are able to see and hear the caller, and the caller can see you but not hear you
Switch cameras (from front to main camera)	Tap ICON
Use another app during a FaceTime call	Press the Home Button
End FaceTime call	Tap ICON

Using the Contacts List

1 Tap the **Contacts** icon on the **Home Screen**

2 Flick up or down till you find the contact you wish to call

3 Select the action you wish to take, e.g. send text message, phone the contact

Add photo to contact

If you want to assign a photo to a contact, find the photo you want to use (or take one of the person) and tap **Assign to Contact**. This means that you get a more personalized phone call, instead of just seeing a name or a number on the screen.

Using the Favorites List

People you call regularly can be added to your favorites list. This is the first icon (from the left) when you open the phone application.

To add someone to your favorites list:

1 Open **Contacts**

2 Select the contact you wish to add

3 Tap **Add to Favorites**

Don't forget

Add the contacts you call most to your Favorites List.

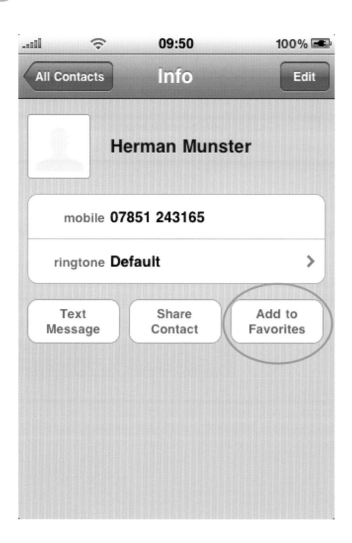

53

Recents List

Recent calls you have made or missed are listed under Recents.

Missed calls

- These are in the **Missed** list and are listed in red
- **All** shows the calls received and missed
- Calls made are shown by the icon ℃
- Calls received are shown without an icon

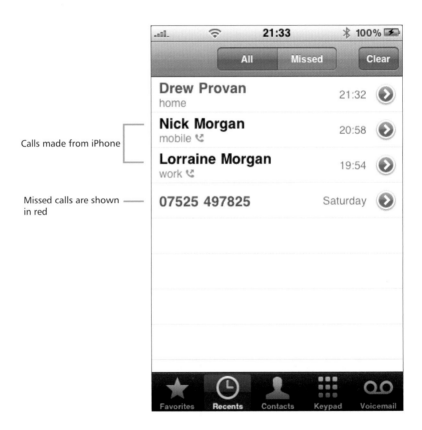

Calls made from iPhone

Missed calls are shown in red

To return a call using Recents list
From the names shown in the Recents list, simply tap the name of the person you wish to call.

Answering Calls

When you receive a call the iPhone will either ring or vibrate, depending on your iPhone settings. If the iPhone is locked, you will see the name of the caller on the screen and you will need to slide the **Answer** button to the right. If the iPhone is unlocked when the call comes in, you will be given the option to **Answer** or **Decline** (and send to voicemail).

This is what you see if a call comes in and your iPhone has locked itself.

You need to **Slide** the green button to the right in order to answer the call.

To send to VoiceMail, hit the **ON/OFF** button at the top.

This is what you see if the iPhone has not locked.

You can either **Answer** and talk to the caller or **Decline** and the caller will be directed to your VoiceMail.

To avoid answering a call, **tap** a volume button once. The iPhone will be silent but the caller will think the iPhone is still ringing and the call will go to VoiceMail.

Answering a Second Call

But what happens if you are actually on a call and a second call comes through? Maybe you want to speak to the second caller rather than have them go through to Voicemail?

You have a few options here:

You can decline to answer the second call — if you ignore the new incoming caller he or she will be directed to your Voicemail.

You can put the first call on hold (explain to them that you are going to do this). Press the **Hold Call + Answer** button on the screen. You can move back and forward between the two calls, putting one on hold each time.

Perhaps the simplest way is to end the first call and answer the second. Simple press **End Call + Answer**, the current call will end, and you will be connected to the second caller.

This is what you see if you are on a call and a second call comes in (providing Call Waiting is ON).

You can ignore or put the first caller on hold and take the second call.

When a third call comes in you can ignore or end the call on hold and answer the third caller.

Or you can end the call you are taking and answer the third caller.

Missed Calls

It happens to all of us from time to time: the boss calls and somehow you managed to miss it. If your iPhone was locked when he called, you can see at a glance that he has called.

You can find out exactly when he called by looking at the missed calls list.

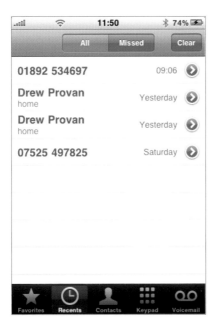

Make the Most of Contacts

The Contacts application on the iPhone lets you call someone, send them an SMS or MMS, email them, and assign them specific ringtones.

Add someone to Contacts

- If someone calls and they are not in your Contacts list why not add them to your list?

- Click the arrow to the right of their number

Here is a missed call (you can see it was missed at 12.09).

To add that person to your Contacts, tap **Create New Contact**, add their First and Last names, and then hit **Save**.

Adding Contacts

- Tap the **Contacts** app to open and click the **+** symbol

- Tap the **First Last** name field

- The cursor will be in the First box — add their first name

- Tap the **Last** box and add their second name

- Tap **Company** if you want to add their company

- Tap **Save**

- This will take you back

- Tap the arrow **>** next to add new phone to add a cell or other phone number

- Work your way through the rest of the fields

- When you are finished hit **Done**

Deleting Contacts

This is much easier:

1 **Tap** the contact you wish to remove

2 Once their details are loaded tap **Edit** at the top right

3 Scroll down to the bottom of the screen and tap **Delete Contact**

4 That's it!

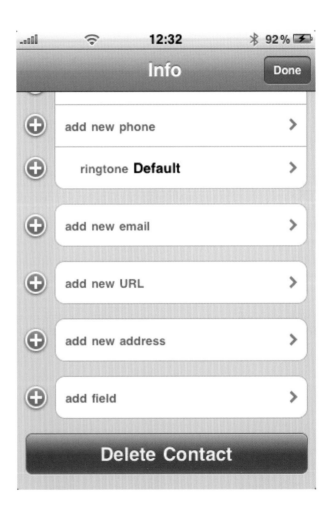

Importing Data from a PC

Most of us prefer to manage and edit our contacts using a computer, rather than the iPhone, because we have a real keyboard and it's easier using the computer. PC users will probably have their contacts in Outlook or Outlook Express. All this contact information can be synchronized with the iPhone each time it is plugged in to the PC.

1 Connect the iPhone to the PC

2 Make sure iTunes is open

3 Go to the **Info** tab

4 Make sure the **Sync contacts from** shows Outlook

5 The **All** contacts radio button should be filled

6 If you keep your contacts grouped, select the **groups** you wish to sync with the iPhone

7 Click **Apply** and the contacts will be synced between the PC and the iPhone (two way)

8 This will happen each time you connect the iPhone to the PC

Importing Data from a Mac

This is similar to the PC method except the Mac uses Address Book to store its contact data, rather than Outlook.

Direct sync with the Mac

1 Connect iPhone to Mac

2 On iTunes click the **Info** tab

3 Ensure **Sync Address Book Contacts** is checked

4 If you want to sync only specific **groups**, check the ones you want to sync

5 Click **Apply**

Now your contacts will be synchronized each time you plug the iPhone into the Mac. But there is another way to keep things in sync, and it is cable-free! However, you do need a MobileMe account. This is not a Mac-specific service so PC users can subscribe to MobileMe as well.

Cloud Syncing with MobileMe

MobileMe is a service provided by Apple, which requires an annual subscription (but you can try it for 60 days for free *http://www.apple.com/mobileme*). MobileMe provides cloud space so you can let your Mac or PC upload your calendar, contacts and notes to a remote server. This communicates wirelessly with your iPhone, keeping all these functions totally in sync.

MobileMe control panel

In the Apple System Preferences, and in PCs in the Control Panel window, you will find the MobileMe control panel. If it's not there you can download it from Apple.

Apple MobileMe control panel | Vista MobileMe control panel

Configure your MobileMe account

- Double click the **control panel**
- Enter your **username** and **password**
- Select what to sync wirelessly, and the frequency of syncing
- That's it, the whole sync process will take place without you having to do anything more

Make Calls Using Headphones

You don't have to hold the iPhone to your ear each time you want to make a call. It's often more convenient to use the headphones. This means you can keep the phone on the desk and make notes during the call.

The headphones are very sophisticated, the right cord contains a white rectangular button which is useful when listening to music, but they are also great for making calls.

How to use the headphones

The is the middle of the controller

Beware

You can use third party headphones with the iPhone but it is likely you will lose some functionality.

Make a phone call	Dial as normal and speak normally. You will hear the caller via the headphones and they will hear your voice, which is picked up by the inbuilt microphone
Answer a call	Click the middle of the control button once
Decline a call	Press the middle of the controller and hold for ~2 seconds (you will hear 2 low beeps to confirm)
End call	Press the middle of the controller once
If already on a call and you wish to switch to an incoming call and put current call on hold	Press the middle button once to talk to caller 2 (and press again to bring caller 1 back)
Switch to incoming call and end the current call	Press and hold the middle of the controller for ~2 seconds (you will hear 2 low beeps to confirm)
Use Voice Control to dial the number	Press and hold the middle button

Using the Bluetooth Earpiece

Instead of using the headphones you can buy Bluetooth headsets. These are fitted into one ear and you can wander around with them in place, taking calls while having both hands free.

Pairing the Bluetooth headset

Bluetooth is a form of wireless and a link must be made between the Bluetooth headset and the iPhone. The Apple Bluetooth headset (*shown below*) comes with a special charger, into which you can plug the iPhone and the Bluetooth headset. The headset and iPhone are automatically paired. If you plan to use a 3rd party Bluetooth headset you will need to pair these manually.

Status light   Button

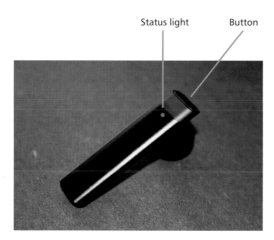

Manual pairing of 3rd party headset to iPhone

● Switch on the iPhone Bluetooth

● Make sure the headset is discoverable

● On the iPhone choose **iPhone Bluetooth headset** and enter the PIN 0000

Use the Bluetooth headset to make calls

Decline a call	Press the button for ~1 second, until you hear a beep
Switch to an incoming call and put current call on hold	Press the button
Switch to incoming call and end the current call	Press the button for ~1 second, until you hear a beep

Call Forwarding

Sometimes you need to forward calls from your iPhone to another phone, for example, if you are somewhere with no cell phone coverage. This is pretty straightforward.

Setting up call forwarding

- Go to **Settings** > **Phone** > **Call Forwarding**

- Slide the **Call Forwarding** slider to the right (**ON**)

- You will be asked for the number you wish to use

- When you no longer need to have your calls forwarded, go back and switch it off

Hot tip

Activate call forwarding if you cannot access the iPhone. You could forward to a landline or your PA.

Conference Calls

This allows you to talk to more than one person at a time and is much like making conference calls using a landline.

Make a conference call

1 Make a call

2 Tap the **Add Call** icon on the screen

3 The first call is put on hold

4 Tap **Merge Calls**

5 Now everyone can hear each other

6 Repeat until up to 5 people are on the same call

Visual Voicemail

This is a fantastic way to retrieve voicemail. No longer do you have to listen to irrelevant messages in order to hear the one you want. With Visual Voicemail you can tap the message you want to hear, and you can listen to that message and that message only.

To retrieve Visual Voicemail

Hot tip

Visual Voicemail makes it very easy to listen to specific voicemail messages.

- Tap the **phone** icon at the bottom of the screen

- Tap the **Voicemail** icon at the far right

- View the voicemail messages

- **Tap** the one you want to hear

- To listen again, tap the **Play** icon

- If you want to listen to an earlier part of the message, **drag the progress slider to the left**

- You can call the caller back by tapping **Call Back**

- You can tap the arrow to the right of the message and add the caller to your Contacts list, or add them to the favorites list

What happens if Visual Voicemail is not available?

This sometimes happens but it's easy to get your voicemail:

Beware

Sometimes you cannot access Visual Voicemail (poor network signal). To retrieve your voicemails tap and hold "1" on the keypad.

- Tap **Phone** > **Keyboard**

- Press and hold the **1** key

- Retrieve your messages

Press and drag slider to LEFT to hear earlier section of voicemail

Customizing Your Greeting

When people get through to your voicemail they will hear a standard greeting, courtesy of your phone provider. Why not leave your own personalized greeting — that way people will be sure they have got through to the correct number.

Create a greeting

1 Select **Phone** from the Home Screen

2 Tap **Voicemail**

3 Tap **Greeting** at the top left of the screen

4 Choose **Custom**

5 Tap **Record** to record your outgoing message

6 Tap **Stop**

7 Make sure the **Custom** option is checked if you wish to use the message you have just recorded

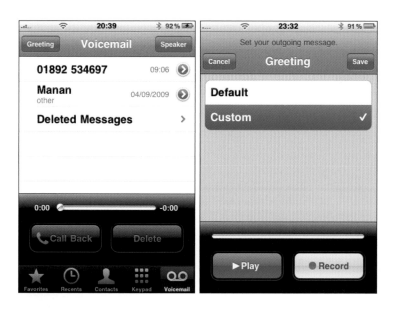

Call Waiting

What is the value of call waiting? If call waiting is switched off, and someone phones you while you are on a call, they will be put straight through to voicemail. However, if call waiting is activated, they will know your line is busy and can wait till you are off the call. Or you can answer their call and put the first caller on hold.

- Go to **Settings** > **Phone**

- Tap **Call Waiting** >

- Slide the **OFF** button to the **ON** position

iPhone Usage Data

How many SMS messages do you have left this month? Or talk minutes? There are times when you need to monitor your usage, since exceeding your limits on your contracted allowance will cost you extra.

How can you check how much you have used?
The iPhone has Usage data under **Settings** > **General** > **Usage**. The information here is very limited and it does not tell you what you have used, or have left, in this month's cycle.

Third party applications
There are a number of apps that can track your monthly usage. These include *Optus Mobile Usage* (for the US) and *Allowance* for the UK. Other countries will have their own specific apps.

iPhone 3G usage screen

Beware

If you exceed your monthly allowance on the iPhone you will be charged extra.

Third Party Apps for Usage

mobile usage

This works with AT&T in the US.

Allowance

This works with O_2 in the UK.

Other countries will have alternative apps to help users monitor their data usage.

3 Messaging

Sending text and multimedia messages is no longer a chore. The iPhone carries out these functions effortlessly.

SMS (Text) Messaging

Loved by teenagers the world over, but disliked by older cell phone users, SMS messaging is one of the most frequently used functions of any mobile device.

The problem has been that adults dislike the texting language used (e.g. C U L8R) but find entering full words cumbersome on traditional cell phones.

The iPhone has changed all that. Now, a full QWERTY keyboard, albeit a virtual touchscreen version, has made texting so much easier.

Hot tip

You can now send SMS and MMS messages to multiple recipients.

Sending a simple text message

1 Tap the **Messages** icon on the Home Screen

2 Tap the **new SMS** icon at the top right of the screen

3 Enter a **recipient name** or a phone number at the top

4 Add any other names if you wish to send to more than one person

5 Go to the **text box** at the bottom and enter your message

6 Hit **Send**

7 The progress bar will show you the status of the message

8 Once sent, the message will appear in a green speech bubble

9 Once the recipient replies, you will see their message below yours in a white speech bubble

10 You can send and receive many texts from the same person, and retain the messages for future use. You can also send them another SMS at any time by tapping the Messages icon and scrolling through your list of messages

How many messages can Messages store?

For each person you text, the app will keep the last 50 messages. If you want to see more than this you need to scroll to the top and tap Load Earlier Messages.

Choose recipient

Their name appears in the To: box

Type message

Hit send. Progess bar shown

If SMS Message Fails

Sometimes things go wrong, maybe you entered a wrong digit, and the message does not get sent. You have the option of retrying. You can also check the contact details and amend the number there.

Send Texts to Multiple Recipients

The Messages app allows you to send texts to more than one person. You can also send texts to groups of individuals.

Send SMS to multiple recipients

1 Type the **name** of the first recipient

2 A shaded block surrounds their name

3 Tap the **To:** field again and add a second name

4 Repeat this till all recipients are added

Tap after each entry
to add other names

Text Message Sounds

Some people like silent texts, others prefer to feel a vibration, but many people like to hear their text messages arrive on the iPhone.

Hot tip

Assign SMS messages a specific sound so you know you have received an SMS.

This is easy to set up

1 Tap **Settings**

2 Go to **Settings** > **Sounds**

3 Tap **New Text Message**

4 Select the **sound** you want from the list

5 Or you can check **None**

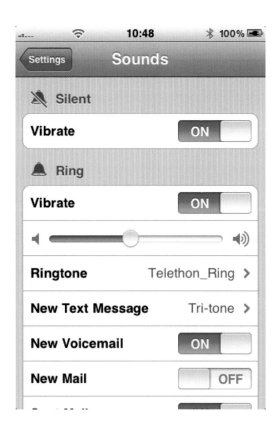

Removing Text Conversations

For privacy, most people remove their text message conversations. You can delete the entire conversation — each and every entry — or you can delete parts of the conversation. It is difficult to save your conversations, but there is a workaround.

Deleting the entire conversation

1 Open up the text message

2 Tap **Edit**

3 **Click the red icon** with the white bar through the center (this deletes the conversation)

4 Alternatively, you can avoid opening the message by simply **sliding your finger across from left to right**, a Delete icon will appear — press **Delete**

Deleting parts of a conversation

1 Open a text with multiple entries

2 Click **Edit**

3 **Tap the speech bubbles** you wish to delete (a red circle with a white check inside will appear)

4 Tap **Delete** at the bottom of the screen

Saving a conversation

1 With the text message conversation window open press the **Home Button** and the **On/Off** button together

2 This will take a snapshot which is saved to your photos

3 You can download to your computer later

Sending MMS Messages

The iPhone can send more than just plain boring text messages. MMS means Multimedia Message Service, which is basically a means of sending images, including video, to a recipient, rather than a simple SMS message. Each MMS counts as 2 SMS messages, so be careful how many you send.

To send an MMS

1 Tap **Messages** and tap **New**

2 Enter the **name** of the recipient

3 **Click the camera icon** (to the left of the text box) and Take Photo or Video or Choose Existing

4 You will then see your photo albums

5 **Choose the picture or video** you want to send

6 The picture will appear in the message box

7 Type your text message to accompany the picture or video

8 Hit **Send**

Tap the camera icon if you want to take a picture to send as an MMS

Choose recipient

Take photo/video or use existing

Tap image

Confirm by pressing Choose

Picture in text box

Add text and send

Other Messaging Clients

There are several other ways of messaging someone. Many of these allow you to send messages in real time, and you can talk by typing responses with the keypad. This type of instant messaging has been in use for several years on the computer. Examples include Microsoft Live Messenger, Skype, Yahoo Messenger, iChat, and many others.

On the iPhone there are several apps that let you message friends and colleagues. Here we will cover:

Hot tip

Skype lets you chat to friends and call them for free.

Skype

Fring

Using Skype

1 **Get yourself a Skype account** using your computer (*www.skype.com*)

2 **Download the free iPhone Skype app** from the App Store

3 Open the app and log in using your registered **Username** and **Password**

4 Your **Contacts List** will be displayed. You can choose to see only those online (makes the list shorter)

5 **Tap** the contact

6 You choose to **Call** or **Chat**

My profile page

Some of my contacts

Choose to Call or Chat

Press Call and this appears

Start chatting. Enter text ...

then hit Send

(I was chatting to to the Skype Test Call rather than a real contact, but it is more fun talking to real people!)

Fring

Why would you need another messaging application? Well, Fring has the benefit of allowing you to log in to several messaging clients (MSN Messenger, ICQ, SIP, Google Talk, Twitter, Yahoo and AIM) — all at once. This means you can see all your friends who use these services and you don't have to open and close different programs to talk to different people.

Using Fring

1 **Download the Fring app** from the App Store and launch the app

2 Enter your **login details** for any of the services listed

3 **Log in to Fring** — the Fring icon will be gray initially (while it logs you in) then will go green when online

4 **Scroll** down the contacts list to find a contact online

5 **Tap** their name and choose whether to chat (using text) or call (using voice)

6 Even if they are offline (gray icon) or idle (orange icon) you can still send a text message which they will see on their home screen

Using Fring to make calls

Choose the country you wish to call

Make cellular calls

List of your contacts

Past chats or calls

Go to recent chats

Using Fring to chat in real time

Green means
you are online

Gray means
the contact is
offline

Fring let's you use all these!

Contacts list

Choose to Call or Chat

Press Call and this appears

Start chatting. Enter text ...

then hit Send

Live Links

When you send a text message, an email, or use a social networking app where text is inserted, you can add phone numbers, web URLs and email addresses. The recipient can then click on these to return the call, visit a website, or send an email.

Hot tip

URLs, email addresses and phone numbers in messages, web pages and emails are live and can be tapped to call the number, view other web pages or send emails.

SMS with telephone number

Tap the phone number to call the number. You can tell it's a live link because the numbers are blue and the phone number is underlined

SMS with email address

Clicking here will bring up a new blank email so you can send an email to this address

Live links in emails

If you send an email to someone and include a website, email address or URL these are also clickable.

Clicking here opens Safari and takes you to the URL in the email

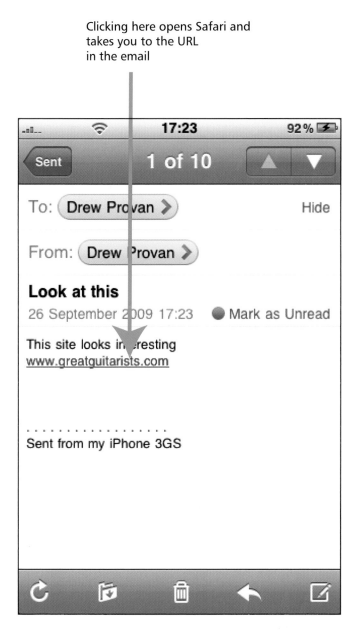

Live Links in Safari

Live links to phone numbers and email addresses don't end with Mail. You can use phone numbers in Safari. If you see a number you want to dial on a web page, put your finger on the number and keep your finger there until a box pops up showing you the various options.

You can:

- Call the number

- Send a text message

- Create a new contact

- Add to an existing contact

1 Put your finger on the number and keep it there

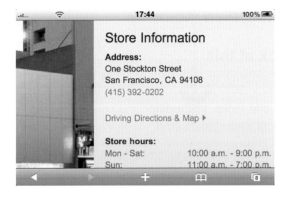

2 You will see the various options

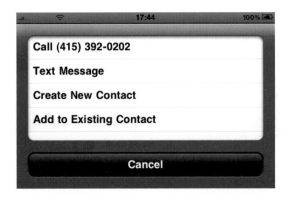

4 Audio & Video

The iPhone is a workhorse but is also a fun device, able to play audio and video just like an iPod. Here we will explore how to get content onto the iPhone and how to use Voice Control to tell your iPhone what you want to hear.

The iPod App

Tap the iPod app icon to open it

Don't forget

If you don't like the way the various functions are shown on the iPod you can change these. Go to iPod > More > Edit

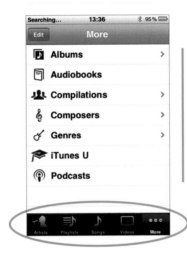

Under the More tab you can view by Album, Audiobooks, Compilations, Composers, Genres, iTunes U, and podcasts

You can view the iPod audio by Artist, Playlist, Songs, Videos or More ...

This view shows the iPod content by Composer

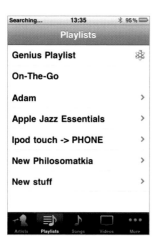

This view shows the iPod content by Playlists

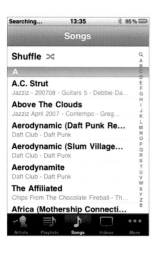

This view shows the iPod content by Songs

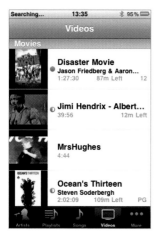

Here we can see some of the videos on the iPod

Play Audio on the iPod

1 Tap **iPod** icon on the dock

2 Tap **Artists** if you want to search this way, or choose **Playlists** or **Songs**

3 **Tap** the name of the artist

4 **Choose** the album you want to hear

5 You can always browse using **Cover Flow** if you can't decide what to play

6 **Tap** the first track (top of the screen) to play the tracks in order

Hot tip

Hold your iPhone in landscape mode to activate Cover Flow.

Flick up & down till you find what you want

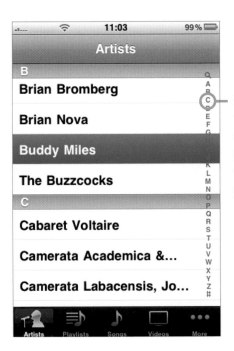

Or tap the letter of the artist you want to play

Tap *Coldplay*. You then move to the Albums view. **Tap** *X&Y*.

You can then see the tracks. **Tap** *Square One* (first track). The speaker icon shows you which track is currently playing.

Useful iPod Controls

Repeat, Genius, Shuffle and Scrubber Bar

This is useful for setting albums to repeat, to listen in random order (Shuffle), to see how far through a track you are and rewind (Scrubber Bar), and to create a Genius playlist

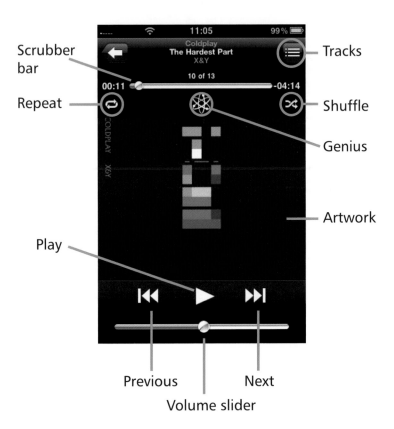

Scrubber bar

Tracks

Repeat

Shuffle

Genius

Artwork

Play

Previous

Next

Volume slider

Shuffle

Tap the Shuffle icon (blue when on, white when off).

Progress bar

To see how long the track is, and how far through you are, tap the cover of the album.

Repeat

You can repeat a song or album by tapping the Repeat icon. This is white if *off*, blue if *on*. You can set the audio to repeat once, twice, or endlessly (why would you want to repeat a track endlessly?).

Shuffle

You can listen to your audio in random order by tapping the Shuffle icon. Like Repeat, when Shuffle is on the icon turns blue. If you want to switch Shuffle off, tap the icon again.

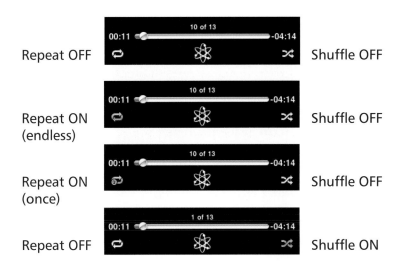

Repeat OFF — Shuffle OFF

Repeat ON (endless) — Shuffle OFF

Repeat ON (once) — Shuffle OFF

Repeat OFF — Shuffle ON

The figure above shows the various combinations for Repeat and Shuffle. In the third example, Repeat is set to *once* — shown by the 1. If you tap again, it will show a 2. If no number is shown the repeat is *endless*.

Shake to Shuffle

You can shuffle the tracks simply by shaking the iPhone.

Don't forget Cover Flow

The iPod app on the iPhone shows Cover Flow just like iTunes!

Turn the iPhone to landscape mode in Album, Song and other modes and you see Cover Flow in action

Flick through the Albums till you find what you want

View the Audio Tracks

Sometimes you want to see what tracks are available, while you are listening to audio.

While viewing the album artwork screen:

1 **Tap the small bullet list** icon at the top right of the screen

2 The album cover flips to show audio tracks available

3 To get back to the main screen again, **tap the Album Artwork icon** at the top right

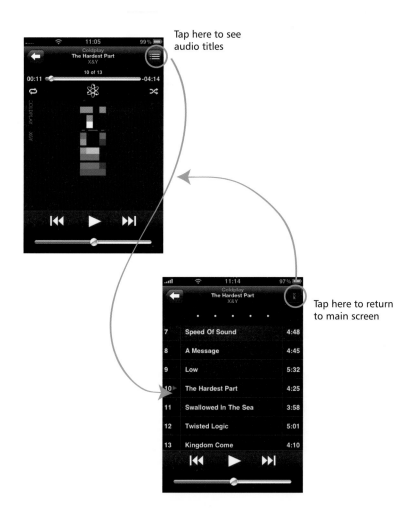

Tap here to see audio titles

Tap here to return to main screen

Adjusting the Volume

There are several ways of increasing or decreasing the audio volume.

Headphones
Use the **+** and **–** on the headset.

Volume control switch on iPhone
Use the physical volume control on the iPhone.

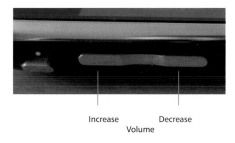

Increase   Decrease
Volume

From iPod screen
Move the circle right (increase volume) or left (to decrease).

Control the iPod from within any app
You don't need to quit an app just to see the iPod controls — just double tap the home button.

Hot tip

Even when you are using another app, you can still access your iPod controls by clicking the Home Button twice.

Search for Audio

Sometimes you can't see the music or artist you are looking for. Hit the search tool at the top right of the iPod screen and type the name of the artist, album, song, podcast, or whatever you are looking for.

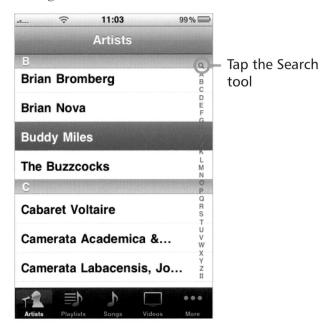

Tap the Search tool

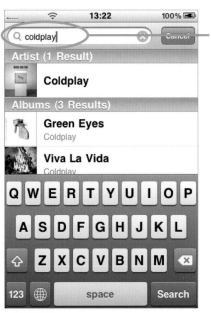

Enter your search terms here

Playlists

Playlists and Smart Playlists are very useful, especially if the music on your Mac or PC will not physically fit onto the iPhone. Making playlists, and choosing to sync specific playlists, helps you decide what music to sync to the iPhone.

In iTunes

1 Choose **File** > **New Playlist**

2 **Name** the playlist

3 From the Music window, **select and drag** the songs you want to add to the new playlist

4 **Drag** the audio files to the playlist

5 When the iPhone is plugged into the Mac or PC, go to the Music pane and **check** the playlists you want to sync to the iPhone

This does *not* move the original files — but it provides *links* to the originals.

Beware

Chances are your music, video, photos etc. will not all fit on the iPhone. You need to design smart playlists that sync selected music, video and photos to the iPhone.

Sync Specific Playlists

To sync specific playlists with the iPhone you need to choose the playlists to sync, from the settings in the iTunes window, when your iPhone is plugged into the Mac or PC.

1 Plug the iPhone into the computer

2 Click **iPhone** in iTunes window

3 Select **Music** pane

4 Make sure sync is set up for **selected** music, artists and genres

5 **Choose** which playlists to sync

6 To avoid hearing the same music over and over, change the playlists you sync every now and again

Ensure "Selected Playlists" is checked

Check each playlist you wish to sync

Hit Apply

Smart Playlists

There is an easier way to get music onto your iPhone. Instead of making playlists, and choosing which songs to add to the iPhone, you can design Smart Playlists. These are playlists which are predefined to contain specific items of music or other audio.

Make a Smart Playlist

1 From iTunes choose **File** > **New Smart Playlist**

2 A setup window with Smart Playlist rules will open

3 **Choose a rule**, such as Album rating = 5 ★

4 In the **Rating** column of iTunes, rate the music you want to add to the Smart Playlist

5 To remove music from the playlist, adjust the rating so it is no longer 5 ★

Hot tip

Use the star rating system to create smart playlists.

Don't forget to name the Smart Playlist!

Watching Video

The iPhone is a great video player. The video controls are located within the iPod app.

1   Tap the **iPod** app to open it

2   Tap **Videos**

3   **Scroll** through the available videos

4   **Tap** the video you wish to watch

5   The playback screen will automatically rotate to landscape

6   **Adjust** volume, rewind, change language and other features using the controls which are shown below

7   If you want to stop, simply press the **Play/Pause** button and it will save your place

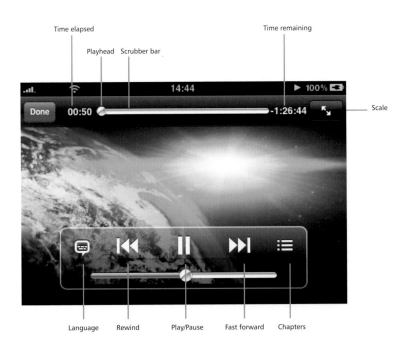

Time elapsed

Time remaining

Playhead   Scrubber bar

Scale

Language   Rewind   Play/Pause   Fast forward   Chapters

Language and Chapters

Adjust the language by tapping the Language icon. If the audio is available in multiple languages these will be shown.

Video DVDs do not always include every language and it's best to check the available languages by loading the DVD on your computer or DVD player first.

Check the languages available for your DVD (by checking the options on a conventional DVD player) before converting for the iPhone, in case your language is not available.

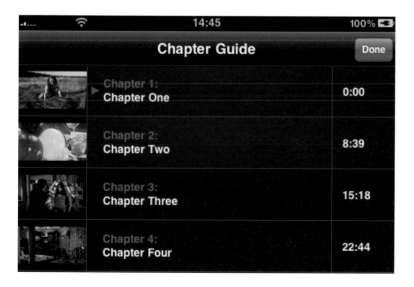

Other Video Icons

Next to the videos you will see small circles which may be wholly filled, partly filled or absent. This tells you how much of each video you have previously viewed. If you stopped watching a video half way through, the circle will be half white and half blue.

Hot tip

The icons next to the video title show you whether a video is unviewed, partially viewed or completely viewed.

Filled circle means the video has not been viewed

This video has been half watched

This video has been fully watched

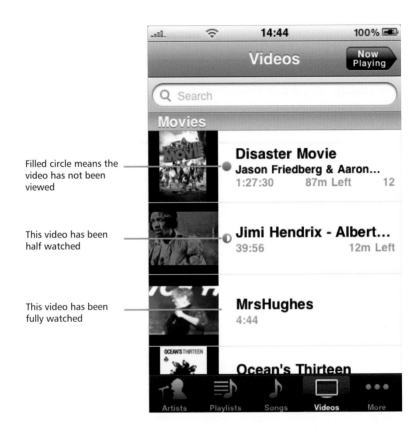

Where to Obtain Videos

You have a few ways of getting videos on your iPhone:

- Home movies, either using a camcorder or the iPhone itself

- Convert your purchased DVDs to iPhone format

- Buy or rent movies from the iTunes store

iTunes store

Select the video you wish to purchase or rent. Once downloaded it will be added to the Movies window in iTunes. When you sync your iPhone choose the movies you wish to sync.

Convert Your DVDs

There are several programs available for Mac and PC that will convert purchased DVDs into an iPhone-friendly format.

Handbrake

This is an open source application for Mac. Simply put your commercial DVD in the Mac optical disk drive, open Handbrake and choose the format for the save. There is an iPhone-specific video format available.

Once converted, the video should be dropped onto the Movies tab of iTunes. In the iPhone Video tab make sure this video is checked so that the next time you sync the iPhone the video will be copied to the iPhone.

Hot tip

Handbrake for the Mac is a free DVD converter which has several save options, including iPhone.

Beware

Copying DVDs, even for personal iPhone use, is probably not legal.

PC software for converting DVDs

There are many different programs for the PC, including Roxio Crunch.

Is it legal?

For a variety of reasons some DVDs may not convert properly, possibly through copy protection. In general, the copying of commercial DVDs, even for your own iPhone use, is not necessarily legal.

Podcasts

The iPhone is also great for listening to audiobooks and podcasts.

Go to **More** > **Podcasts**   Tap the one you want to hear

The blue circle denotes a podcast which has not been played.

On-The-Go Playlists

On-The-Go playlists contain audio or video which you might want to hear when you run, or in the car.

To set up the On-The-Go playlist:

1 Go to **iPod** > **Playlists**

2 Tap **On-The-Go**

3 You will see all your audio

4 Tap the **+** icon to add songs

5 If you want to remove or edit the playlist, open the On-The-Go playlist and tap **Edit**

6 Remove any tracks you want. You can also **Clear** the entire On-The-Go playlist

Hot tip

On-The-Go playlists are another form of useful smart playlist.

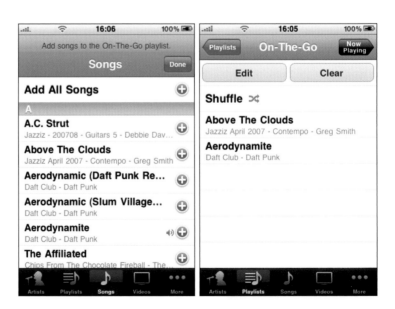

Add your tracks to the On-The-Go playlist. Edit later when you want a different selection.

Genius

Genius is available within iTunes, on iPods and the iPhone. Genius works out what you listen to and can help make playlists based on song types. It works out what music fits well with other music.

For example, let's say you are listening to something jazzy, which you like. Genius can help make a playlist from your music based on the jazz track you are listening to.

Here's how:

1 Open **iPod** and select **Playlists**

2 Tap **Genius**

3 **Choose the song** you want to use as the basis of your Genius playlist

4 If you get bored with this list of songs simply **Refresh**

Hot tip

If you cannot decide what to listen to, click Genius and let the iPhone decide for you.

109

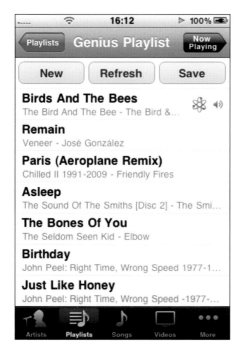

Voice Control with the iPod

Rather than tap your way through finding songs, videos and other audio content, you can tell your iPod what to play using Voice Control. This is a feature *only* available with the iPhone 3GS and 4G (not earlier iPhones).

Beware

Voice Control is only available on the iPhone 3GS and 4G .

Control music playback	Say play or play music. To pause, say pause or pause music. You can also say next song or previous song
Play an album, artist, or playlist	Say play, then say album, artist, or playlist and the name
Shuffle current playlist	Say Shuffle
Find out more about the currently playing song	Say what's playing, what song is this, who sings this song, or who is this song by
Use Genius to play similar songs	Say Genius, play more like this, or play more songs like this
Cancel Voice Control	Say cancel or stop

5 Photos & Video

The iPhone has a built-in camera, and is able to shoot movies as well as still images. In addition, you can even edit your movies directly on the iPhone.

iPhone Camera

The camera in the iPhone can be used for taking still photographs and video.

Camera

Tap to Focus

The iPhone camera can adjust the focus and the exposure — by tapping the screen when taking a picture or shooting video.

Geotagging

The iPhone camera will provide geotagging data, including your geographical coordinates, provided you have switched Location Services on (**Settings** > **General** > **Location Services**).

Beware

Night shots, or scenes with reduced light, often produce poor quality images on the iPhone.

The camera has a resolution of 5 megapixels which is more than enough to take good pictures and video. The poorest results are seen when the lighting is low. Night shots are particularly bad. For best shots make sure there is lots of light around. The 4G model also has a camera flash for the main camera.

Location of camera lens

You will find this on the back of the iPhone at the top left corner. Take care not to scratch the lens, and clean the lens only with the cloth provided.

Main camera lens
Keep it clean!

Still Images Using Main Camera

1 Tap the **camera** icon to load the app

2 The shutter will open to show the image

3 Take care to keep still (place your elbows against your sides to steady your arms)

4 Touch the camera icon towards the bottom of the screen

5 The picture will be visible for a second or two before being dropped into the folder called **Camera Roll**, which you can find by launching the Photos application

6 Take care not to place your finger over the lens

If you want to use the FRONT camera, tap this icon to switch from MAIN to FRONT and take picture in same way as if using MAIN camera

Tap screen to autofocus and automatically adjust exposure (tap the area you want to be the main focal point)

The photo will be added to the Camera Roll — tap here to open

Tap here when you are ready to take the photo

Where are My Pictures?

- Photos and video taken using the camera end up in an album called Camera Roll

- Other pictures you have copied to the iPhone, by checking specific albums for syncing, are shown below the Camera Roll

- Find the photos you want by tapping the library and selecting the image

- You can email and view pictures in your libraries on the iPhone but you cannot delete them (although you *can* delete pictures from the camera roll — these are pictures you have taken using the iPhone camera)

- To remove photos from albums you need to use iTunes

Don't forget

Camera Roll contains the images taken with the iPhone. The other albums listed are those synced from your PC or Mac to the iPhone.

Pictures taken with the camera are in this album

Pictures synced from your computer are here

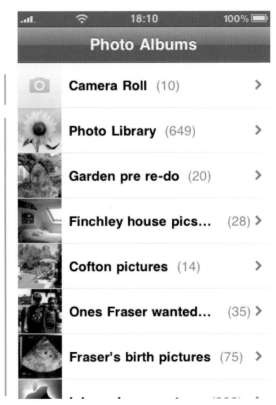

Taking Videos

① **Tap the camera icon** to load the app. The shutter will open to show the image

② **Push the Camera/Video slider** to the right to put the camera into video mode

③ **Touch the camera icon** at the bottom of the screen. To record in High Definition, tap screen and **tap HDR**

④ The Record icon flashes red on and off during filming

⑤ When you have finished, tap the camera icon at the bottom. Your video will be in the Camera Roll Album

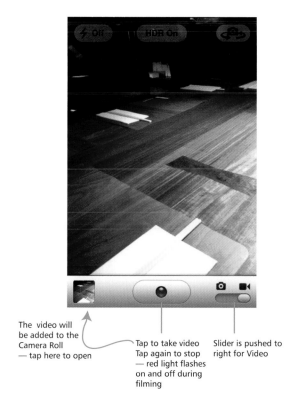

The video will be added to the Camera Roll — tap here to open

Tap to take video Tap again to stop — red light flashes on and off during filming

Slider is pushed to right for Video

Hot tip

Videos are located in the Camera Roll album.

Editing the Video

You can edit the video you have taken on a Mac, PC or directly on the iPhone itself.

1 Tap the **Photos** application

2 Tap **Camera Roll** and locate your video

3 **Tap the video** to open it — the image can be viewed in portrait or landscape, but landscape is easier for trimming

4 **Touch the screen** and the trimming timeline will be shown at the top of the screen

5 Decide what (if anything) you want to trim and drag the sliders on the left and right until you have marked the areas you wish to trim

6 Tap the yellow **trim** icon at the top right of the screen and the unwanted video will be removed

Hot tip

Video editing is now non-destructive which means you can trim your video, but the original video clip is left intact.

Hit trim when you are happy with the edit

Drag to the right   Drag to the left

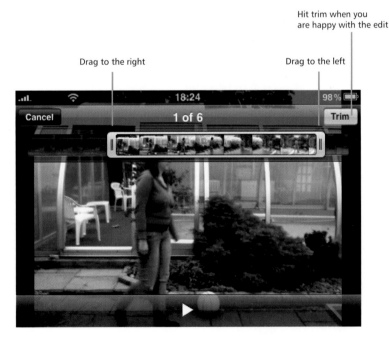

Sharing Photos & Video

You can share photos and videos with friends and colleagues using a number of different methods.

Email

1 Go to **Photos** > **Camera Roll** and locate the photo or video

2 **Tap the icon** on the bottom left and decide whether you want to email or send the photo using MMS

3 Alternatively you can **post** to YouTube or MobileMe

4 You can also **assign** the photo to one of your contacts or use the image as a **wallpaper**. Just tap the relevant icon

Don't forget

As well as editing and watching the video on the iPhone, you can send your video clips to YouTube, MobileMe or MMS to contacts.

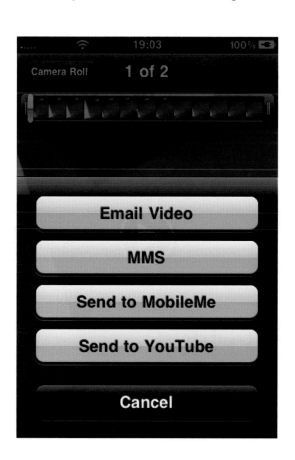

Uploading Your Images

1 **Locate the photo or video** you wish to upload

2 Tap the **Sharing** icon (bottom left)

3 Choose **YouTube** or **MobileMe**

4 You will be prompted for your login name and password

5 Provide these and the image should upload

6 With MobileMe you will need to specify an online album where you want the images stored

7 You will need a MobileMe account (subscription to Apple) and if you intend to use YouTube you will need to set up an account there, too (free)

8 You could always set up a Posterous account (*http://www.posterous.com*) and upload your photos for friends and family to see there

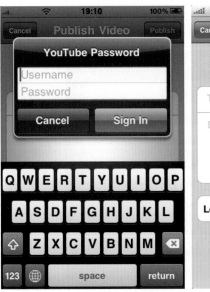 

6 The Standard Apps

Each iPhone comes preinstalled with a core set of applications, which make the iPhone so versatile and useful. In this section we explore each of these apps in turn and show how to get best use out of them.

Calendar

For people who want to get organized, people in business, education and many other sectors, the core applications are: Calendar, Mail, Contacts, Phone and Notes.

These apps integrate well with each other on the iPhone and also the PC and Mac.

Setting up Calendar

Before you start entering data into Calendar, there are one or two settings you should check:

Beware

Make sure your Time Zone is set correctly or all your appointments will be incorrect.

1 Go to **Settings** > **Mail, Contacts, Calendars**

2 Tap **Mail, Contacts, Calendars** to open

3 Scroll down the page till you find **Calendars**

4 Switch **New Invitation Alerts** to ON

5 Choose what to **Sync** (do you want all events or just those for the past 2 weeks, month, 3 months, or 6 months?)

6 Make sure **Time Zone Support** is correct or times on your calendar will be incorrect

7 **Set your default calendar** — when you make new appointments using Calendar this is where the appointments will be added (you can add to another calendar quite easily, though)

8 That's it. Now you can start getting appointments into your Calendar using: iPhone, Apple iCal or Microsoft Outlook on the PC

9 We'll discuss each method in turn, and also look at how to keep your desktop computer and iPhone Calendar in sync at all times

Calendar Views

1 Tap the **Calendar** icon to open the application

2 You will see the **Month View** — if it opens in **Day** or **List**, tap **Month**

3 This shows an overview of the month

4 A black dot means you have an appointment on that day, but it does not tell you how long the appointment is or what it is. But look at the bottom of the screen and you will see what the day's appointments are

5 If you need a detailed view of your appointments, check out the Day view

Last month

Next month

Black dots represent appointments

Today

These are detailed in this window

Tap appointments to view the details

Day View

This provides a more detailed view of your day, showing the times on the left margin, and all your appointments are shown in the colors chosen by you.

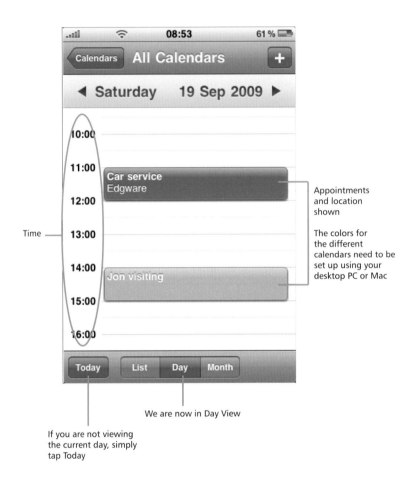

Time

Appointments and location shown

The colors for the different calendars need to be set up using your desktop PC or Mac

We are now in Day View

If you are not viewing the current day, simply tap Today

How to move quickly through the days in Day View

Press and hold the arrows to move backwards quickly...

Or move fowards quickly

List View

Sometimes you want to see all your appointments as a list, rather than browsing through several months' worth of appointments using the other views.

Simply tap List and you will see every appointment, with the earliest at the top and the latest at the bottom.

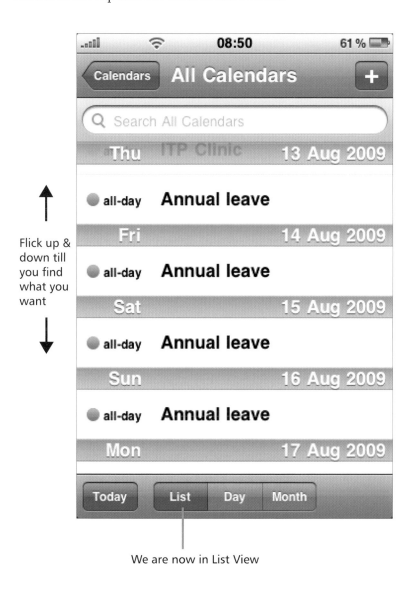

Flick up & down till you find what you want

We are now in List View

Searching Calendar

It's very easy to find appointments using the Search function within Calendar. You can also use Spotlight Search to find appointments.

1 Tap **Calendar** to open

2 Tap **List view**

3 Tap the **search box** for an item, e.g. Car Service. After you enter a few letters the appointments containing those letters will appear below

4 Tap the appointment found to see the details

Don't forget

You can search your calendar using the inbuilt search tool or use Spotlight.

Start typing here

Your results are shown here

Spotlight Search

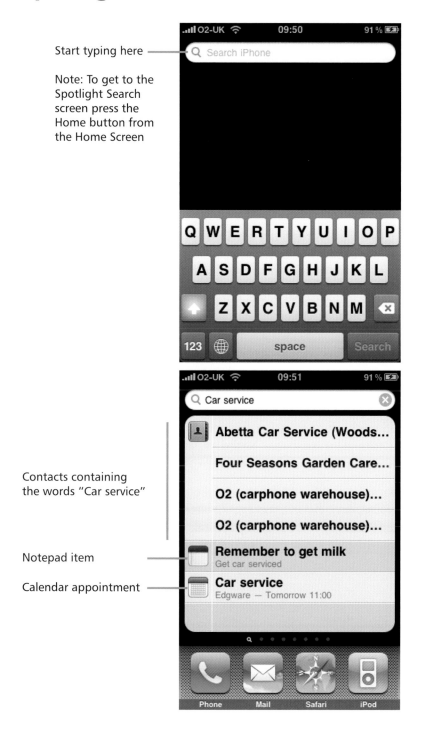

Start typing here

Note: To get to the Spotlight Search screen press the Home button from the Home Screen

Contacts containing the words "Car service"

Notepad item

Calendar appointment

Adding Appointments

Add appointments using iPhone
This is very straightforward.

1   Tap **Calendar** to open

2   You can either go to the day of the appointment you wish to add, or you can simply tap the **+** icon at the top right of the screen

3   Enter **Title**, **Location**, then hit **Done**

4   Enter **start** and **end** time. If the date is not correct, choose the correct date

5   If it **repeats** (e.g. birthdays, anniversaries, etc) enter the frequency

6   If you want an **alert** to appear on the screen, tap the appropriate time for the alert

Multiple calendars
You might want to assign an appointment to a specific calendar, for example work, home, birthdays, vacation, etc. When you make the appointment you will be shown the Calendar tab.

You must decide which calendar the appointment belongs to *now* because, once chosen, you cannot change your mind and alter it on the iPhone. If you do want to switch an event to another calendar you will need to do this in Outlook or iCal. This is an odd feature of the Calendar app, and hopefully Apple will sort this.

Beware

You can edit appointments on the iPhone itself, but you cannot alter the calendar with which the appointment is associated. Choose the correct calendar when you are making the appointment on the iPhone.

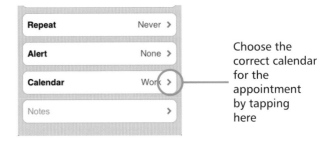

Choose the correct calendar for the appointment by tapping here

Set up new appointment:

Enter details for **Title** and **Location**, tap **Starts/Ends** and enter start and end time for the appointment.

Tap the "+" to add

Enter appointment and location

Tap "Starts/Ends"

Set Start and End time

...cont'd

Next, decide whether you want alerts, the appointment to repeat and which Calendar you wish to contain the appointment.

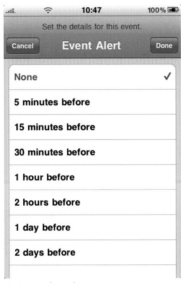

Set up the alert

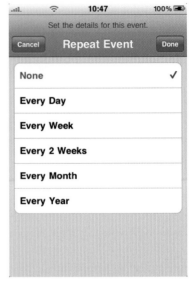

Decide on repeat frequency

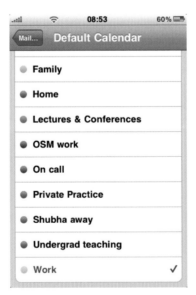

If you have multiple calendars, choose the one you wish the appointment to be associated with

Setting up Multiple Calendars

Why do you need multiple calendars? Well, you might want to keep work and home separate. You could put all your holidays, dental appointments and other personal items into the Home calendar and keep all your business appointments separate.

Many people share their calendars with, for example, their secretaries. You can publish Outlook and iCal calendars online but you don't necessarily want your work colleagues to view all your personal calendar items.

Hot tip

Keep your work and personal calendar information separate by creating separate calendars.

On the Mac

1 Open **iCal**

2 Click the **+** symbol (bottom left)

3 Give your new Calendar a **name**

4 Right click the name of the new calendar and **choose the color**

5 If you only want to see the appointments associated with a specific calendar uncheck those you do *not* want to see

129

Add Appointment to iCal

1 Double click anywhere on the **calendar**

2 Double click the **New Event** box and it will open

3 Give the event a **title** and enter the **location**

4 Check the **All Day** box if it's an all-day event, otherwise leave unchecked

5 Enter **Date** and **Time** of start and end

6 Decide which calendar to associate with the appointment (from the drop-down list)

7 If you want an **alarm** (text, email, open a file, run a script) set it here

8 If you are inviting others to the meeting, use the **Add Invitees** option and enter their email addresses

9 If you want to add **attachments** or make **notes**, add these then hit **Done**

Add Appointment to Outlook

1 Open **Outlook** and **double click** somewhere on the calendar

2 An untitled appointment will open

3 Give it a **Subject** and **Location**

4 Add **Start time** and **End time**

5 Check or uncheck **All Day** box

6 Enter **Notes** and set up **alarm**

7 To associate with a specific calendar, drag the appointment to that calendar name in the left column

8 **Save and close**

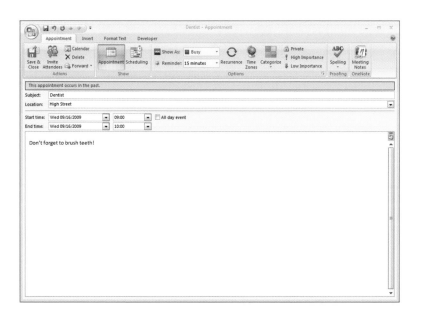

Outlook Multiple Calendars?

iCal overlays multiple calendars very easily but with Outlook there is a tweak you have to use, otherwise you end up with all your separate calendars side by side which makes them very difficult to read.

View in Overlay Mode

1   Make sure all your separate calendars in **Outlook** are checked (left column). If you have 3 calendars you will see all 3 side by side

2   Click the **View in Overlay Mode** and they will all merge!

All calendars are checked but impossible to view!

Click the arrow here to view in Overlay Mode

This gives you an overlaid calendar with all your appointments:

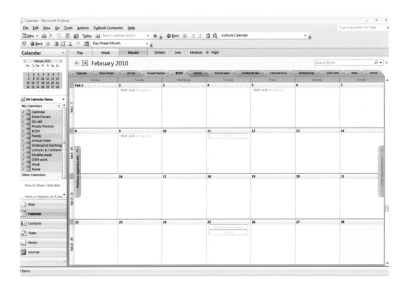

Changing the calendar associated with an appointment?

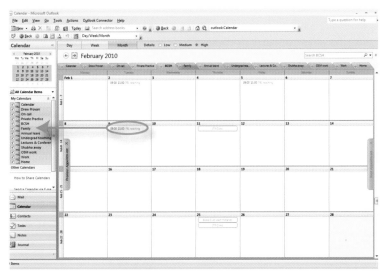

Drag & drop
the appointment
onto the calendar
it should be
associated with

Sync Calendar with PC and Mac

Mac

There are two main ways to sync your calendar information:

- By direct USB connection with the Mac — iTunes will automatically perform a sync unless you have switched this feature off

- Using cloud computing, e.g. MobileMe — this will wirelessly sync all your data (Contacts, Calendars but not Notes)

MobileMe syncing

Hot tip

Calendar data can be synced using a USB connection with your desktop computer, or wirelessly using MobileMe.

1 In the **MobileMe** control panel **select iCal sync**

2 Edit the **settings** to suit your requirements

3 These are shown opposite

Wireless sync on the PC

1 Go to **Control Panels** > **MobileMe**

2 Check the box for **Outlook sync**

USB sync on the PC

1 Under the **Info** panel in iTunes, check the button for **Sync calendars with Outlook**

2 Each time you connect the iPhone to the PC, using USB, automatic syncing will take place

Notes Application

All good PDAs have some kind of note-taking software and the iPhone is no exception. The Notes application can be found on the Home page, but you can move it to wherever you want it. The notes you make can be synced with your desktop computer and we will look at this later.

To make a note:

1 Tap the **Notepad** icon to open the application

2 Tap the **+** symbol to make a new note

3 Tap **Done** when you're finished

4 You will return to the screen showing all your notes

5 You can navigate back and forth through your notes, email them and trash them.

Tap the "+" to make new note

Tap any note to open, read and edit

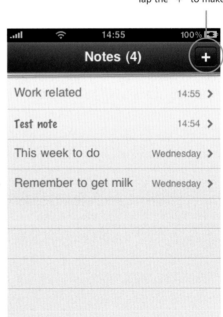

Notes controls

Previous note   Email note   Trash note   Next note

Don't like the default font?
The default iPhone Notes font is Marker Felt (the Test note above uses this font) which many people don't like much. If you don't like it, change it.

Change the font

1   Go to **Settings** > **Notes**

2   Choose the font you prefer

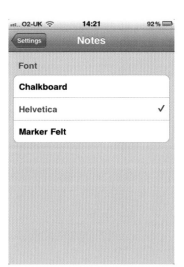

If you don't like the default font in Notes, change it in Settings.

Sync Notes with Computer

On the Mac

No wireless (cloud) computing is available for the Notes application, so you need to set things up in Mail.

You need to click on Notes to see your notes but if you prefer to have notes mixed in with emails, you can check Show Notes in inbox.

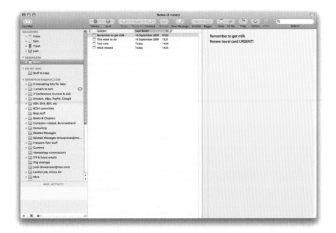

...cont'd

On the PC

No wireless (cloud) computing is available for the Notes application on the PC, so you need to set things up in iTunes.

1 Plug the iPhone into the PC

2 When **iTunes** opens, select the **iPhone** tab in the left column

3 Under the **Info** tab select the **Notes** pane

4 Make sure **Notes** are set to sync with Outlook

5 Syncing will occur each time you plug the iPhone into the PC

6 If you want to stop syncing your notes, **uncheck** the tab

Maps Application

Maps is a great application — it can help you find where you are now, where you want to go, help you plan the route, tell you what direction you are facing and where all the traffic is.

140

Open Maps: You are here!

Tap blue circle to see which way you're facing

Tap lower left corner and drop pin

Pin shows your location

Satellite view

Hybrid view

Finding a route

Tap the Directions button and enter your start and end points.

Maps will calculate a route. It will also tell you how long it will take by car, public transport and by foot.

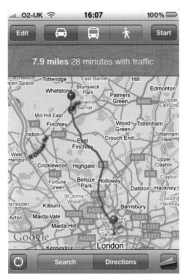

Ok, how about by car?

Plan your route: how long does it take to walk?

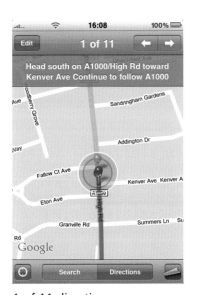

1 of 11 directions screens

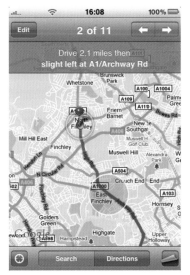

2 of 11 directions screens

Weather Application

This does what it says on the tin: it tells you what the weather is for the next 6 days. You can program the app to show the weather in multiple places. You can also choose between Centrigrade or Fahrenheit.

Tap the "i" and the screen will flip round

Tap the Search box and enter the name of a location. When you find what you want tap it then tap the lower right corner to flip the screen back

Stocks Application

This app makes it easy to see how your stocks and shares are doing, both numerically and graphically.

What's happening on the FTSE 100?

Here is Apple's performance over the past 2 years.

iBooks

This is a "standard" app but won't be on your iPhone by default. You need to go and grab a copy from the app store (free). You will need to have an iTunes account, even to download free books.

The app is very similar to the iPad version, albeit with a smaller screen.

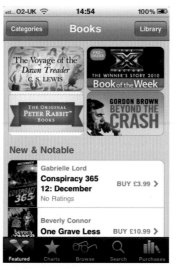

iBooks has 2 main views: Store, which is like iTunes, where you can browse through the various categories of books and download to your iPhone. You will need an iTunes account.

If you tap Library, you will see the books you have downloaded. If you have any PDFs in the library you will see these if you tap PDFs.

Tap Store and you can browse, buy and download book

Library view — Books

Library view — PDF files

Nike + iPod App

This app works with the Nike gadget that fits in your sneakers. When you run, it sends data to your iPhone which is then uploaded to the Nike website when you sync your iPhone using iTunes. If you enjoy running you will find this app indispensable!

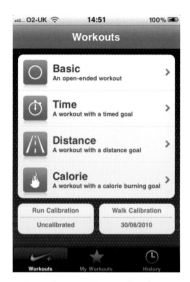
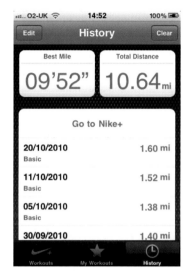

Select the workout, do the run, and view your past runs

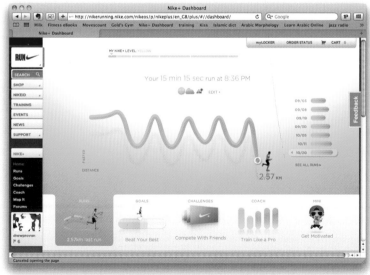

Here is the Nike+ Dashboard showing my runs

Calculator

As expected, this is a fully functioning calculator. You can view a standard calculator if you view in portrait mode. However, if you rotate the screen to landscape, the calculator changes to a scientific calculator.

To access the scientific calculator, turn the iPhone to landscape.

Rotate through 90° to see the scientific calculator:

Clock

This app functions as a clock, alarm, stop watch and timer. You can see what time it is in any city in the world by adding these to your clock screen.

Current time in 4 cities

Tap edit to add or delete locations. Drag up and down

Alarm clock function

Stopwatch

Timer function

Compass

The compass needs to be calibrated before you use it — wave the iPhone in a figure of eight. The needle points to north and you can find your current location by tapping the lower left icon.

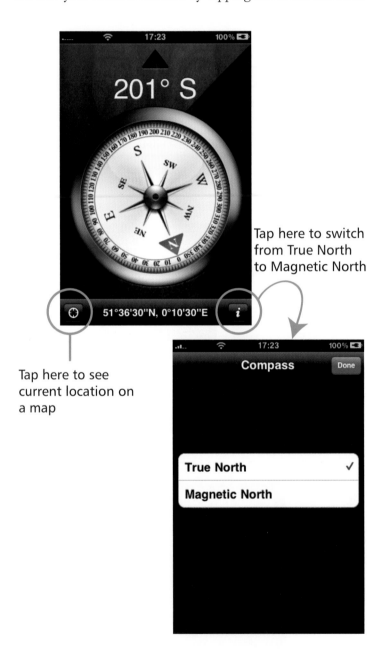

Tap here to switch from True North to Magnetic North

Tap here to see current location on a map

iTunes Store Application

This is the iPhone version of the iTunes store on the Mac or PC. You can buy audio and video content for your iPhone.

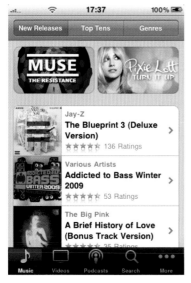

Purchase music

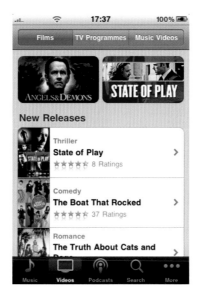

Videos

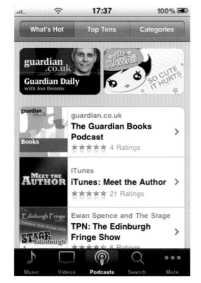

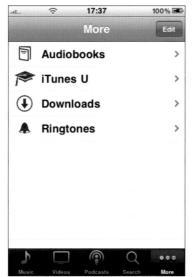

Download free and paid podcasts or audiobooks

YouTube

You can search for YouTube videos, watch then rate and bookmark them, and email them.

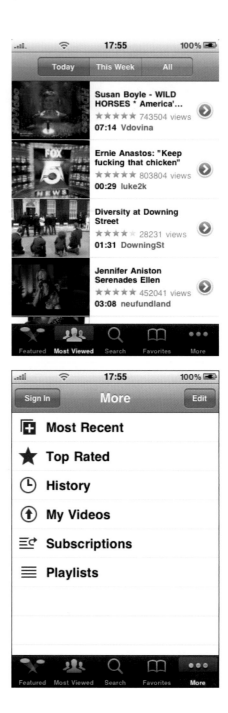

Watch the videos:

Time elapsed

Playhead Scrubber bar

Time remaining

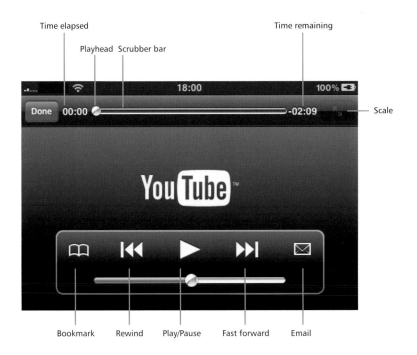

Scale

Bookmark   Rewind   Play/Pause   Fast forward   Email

151

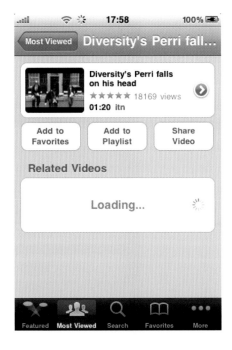

Hot tip

It's easy to share YouTube videos with friends. Locate the video you want then tap "Share Video".

Voice Memos

The iPhone is a great voice recorder. You can make voice notes for yourself then email them to colleagues or yourself to listen to later.

1 Tap **Voice Memos** to open

2 Tap the **Record** icon (it changes to a Pause icon). You will see the time elapsed

3 Pause recording by hitting the **Pause** button

4 If you need to take a call, or use another app, you will see **Recording Paused** on a red bar at the top of the screen. To return to Voice Memos, tap the red bar at the top of the screen

5 When finished, tap the **Stop** button

6 You will then be taken to a screen showing all your voice memos

7 Listen to them on the speaker, using headphones, email them or send them via MMS

8 You can **Trim** the memos if there is unwanted material you wish to remove

Time elapsed

Tap here to Record
Tap again to Pause

Tap here to go
to Voice Memos

Tap here to Stop

Tap home button during recording.
You will then see the Home Page.
To return to the Voice Memo recording
tap the red area

Listen to the recording, or
send it by Email or MMS

Photos

This was covered, in part, in Chapter 5.

Tap Photos to view albums

Tap the album to view it

Move through using arrows
or flick with your finger

You can email, send by MMS,
upload to MobileMe, assign to
contact or use as wallpaper.

Or you can press the play button
and watch a presentation of
all the photos in that album

7 Accessing the Internet

Browsing the web on the iPhone is very easy using Apple's inbuilt browser, Safari. We will look at how to use Safari, save and organize bookmarks and use live links within web pages.

Network Connections

Your iPhone can download data, such as emails and web pages, using a number of different types of connection. Some types of connection are faster than others. In general, Wi-Fi and Bluetooth should be kept off if you are not using them because they use a considerable amount of power.

GPRS
This is a slow network! But often better than nothing.

EDGE
This is a relatively slow connection but is fine for email.

3G
This is a faster connection than EDGE but slower than Wi-Fi.

Wi-Fi connection
Joining a wireless connection will give you fairly fast download speeds. There are many free Wi-Fi hotspots. You can use home Wi-Fi once you enter the password.

Bluetooth
This is a short-range wireless connection, generally used for communication using a Bluetooth headset.

What do the various icons mean?
Look at the top of the iPhone and you will see various icons relating to cellular and other networks.

Beware

Wi-Fi and Bluetooth drain battery power. Switch off when not required.

⚙	GPRS
E	EDGE
3G	3G
📶	Wi-Fi ON with good signal strength
✳	Bluetooth ON
✈	Airplane mode ON
✺	iPhone is busy connecting, or getting mail, or some other task which has not completed

Configuring Networks

Wi-Fi

1 Go to **Settings** > **Wi-Fi**

2 Tap **Wi-Fi**

3 Tap **ON** if it is off

4 Choose a **network** from those listed and enter the password

5 Tap **Ask to Join Networks** if you want to be prompted each time a new network is found. It's generally easier to leave this OFF

6 If you want to forget the network (e.g. maybe you have used one in a hotel), tap the name of the network you have joined, and tap **Forget this Network**

Bluetooth

1 Go to **Settings** > **General** > **Bluetooth**

2 Tap **ON** if it is off

3 Go back and switch off when not needed in order to conserve battery power

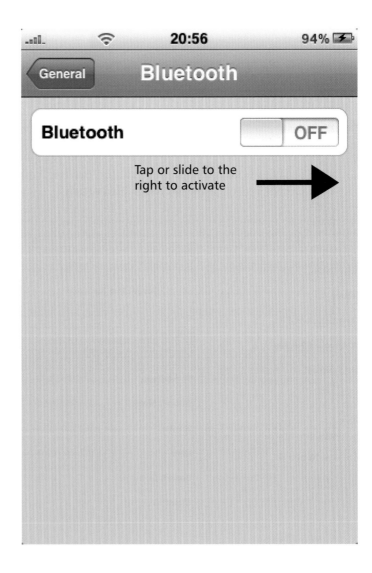

Switch All Networks Off

1 Put the iPhone in **Airplane Mode**

2 Go to **Settings** > **Airplane Mode**

3 Tap **ON** if it is off

4 Use this on the plane or when you want to conserve power

Browse the Internet

Safari is Apple's browser on the Mac and also on the iPhone. It is clean and uncluttered, which makes it ideal for mobile devices such as the iPhone.

1 Tap the **Safari** browser to open it

2 Tap the **address field** to enter the URL

3 Tap **Go**

4 To erase the URL, go to the address field and **tap the cross** which clears the text

5 **Browse** in portrait or landscape

6 To **scroll**, drag your finger up and down the screen

7 To **enlarge** the text, double tap the screen or stretch the text by pushing 2 fingers apart whilst placed on the screen

Don't forget

Enlarge the font by tapping twice on the screen.

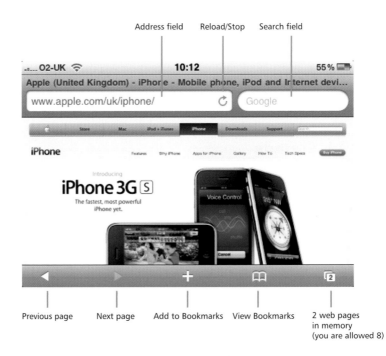

Address field   Reload/Stop   Search field

Previous page   Next page   Add to Bookmarks   View Bookmarks   2 web pages in memory (you are allowed 8)

Safari Bookmarks

You can add, delete, and organize bookmarks in Safari. In addition, you can sync bookmarks between your desktop and iPhone using MobileMe.

This shows the bookmarks in bookmarks folders

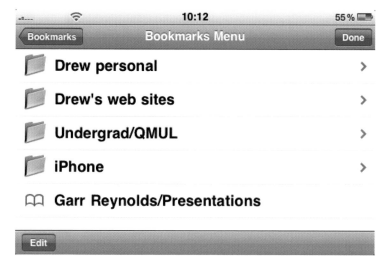

Tap Edit to delete entries, shift up or down and create new folders

To clear History: tap **History**, tap **Clear History**.

Don't forget

Clear your browsing history from time to time to help maintain privacy.

Zooming and Scrolling

Because of the small screen there is a limit to how much you can see of the web page.

Scroll
Place your finger on the screen and drag up or down, and left or right.

Zoom

1 Place your index and middle finger on the screen

2 Push them apart to zoom in

3 Pinch them together to zoom out

To scroll, place your finger on the screen and move the content up and down or side to side

Don't forget

You can also zoom in by placing 2 fingers on the screen and pushing them apart (pull them closer to reduce the size).

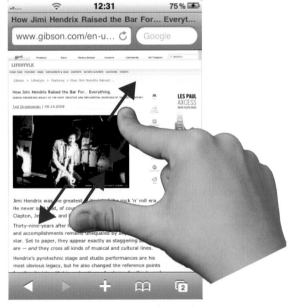

Pinch two fingers while touching the screen (zoom out) or pull your fingers closer together (zoom in) or double tap the screen (enlarge)

Add Web Clip to Home Screen

If you find a site that you want to revisit, but not add to
bookmarks, you can add it to the home screen:

Find the site you want, tap the "+" icon

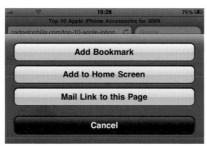

Tap "Add to Home Screen"

Give the link a name

The link is now
on the Home Screen

Move to whichever
location you prefer

Private Browsing

It's a good idea to clear your browsing history and other data from time to time:

1 Tap **Settings** on the Home Screen

2 Locate **Safari**, tap its button

3 Tap **Clear History**, **Clear Cookies** and **Clear Cache**

4 All private browsing data will be erased

5 Alternatively, download a browser that *only* works in private mode from the App Store

6 One example is the app *Privately* — this stores no data so there is nothing to clear later

Hot tip

Third party private browsers (no history or cache retained) are available in the App Store.

Go to **Settings** > **General** > **Safari**
Tap Safari and tap Clear History, Clear Cookies and Clear Cache
by tapping their buttons

Copy Text from Safari

With Copy & Paste you can easily grab text and graphics from Safari and paste into an email or other app.

This can be a bit hit-and-miss, and takes practise.

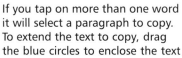

Don't forget

You can copy text and images from web pages and paste into emails or other apps.

Tap screen twice — on the second tap keep finger on the screen. If you tap on one word, it will be selected for copying

If you tap on more than one word it will select a paragraph to copy. To extend the text to copy, drag the blue circles to enclose the text

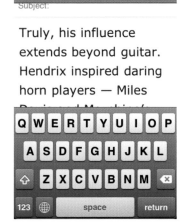

Tap copy, close Safari and open an app such as Mail. Touch the text area and "Paste" will appear. Tap "Paste" to paste the copied text

Tricks

Remove and add Safari pages

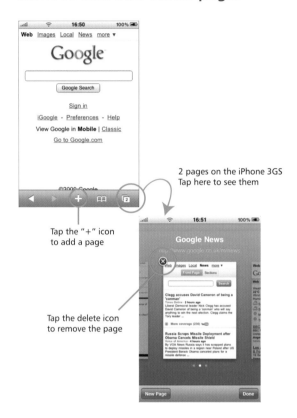

2 pages on the iPhone 3GS
Tap here to see them

Tap the "+" icon
to add a page

Tap the delete icon
to remove the page

Keyboard shortcuts when entering URLs

You don't need to type *.co.uk* or *.com*. On the Safari keyboard, press and hold the *.com* key. Alternatives will pop up (the *.kr* options are showing because the Korean keyboard is active).

Hot tip

You don't have to enter ".com" or ".co.uk" — simply hold down the ".com" key and alternatives will pop up.

Fast Safari Scrolling

You can scroll up and down through web pages in Safari using your finger to flick up and down. But there is a very quick way of getting to the top of any web page.

Tap the time! (this works with text messages too).

Tap the time

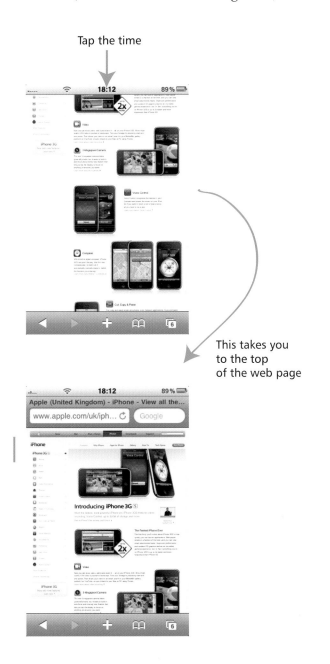

This takes you
to the top
of the web page

Hot tip

Zoom to the top of the browser window by tapping the time at the top of the screen.

Set Default Search Engine

Safari has Google as the default search engine. You may be happy to keep Google or you can change to another search engine.

How to switch to another search engine

Don't forget

You can set your default search engine to Yahoo! or Bing, instead of Google.

1 Go to **Settings** > **Safari**

2 Look for **Search Engine**

3 **Tap** the button and you will see Yahoo! and Bing listed

4 **Choose** either Safari or Yahoo! or Bing

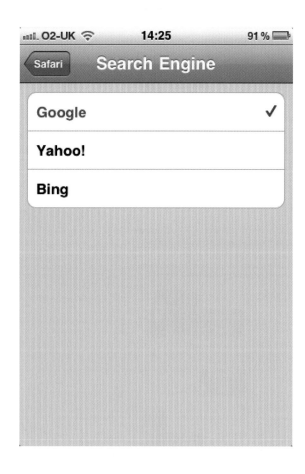

8 Using Email

Most of us spend a great deal of time reading and composing emails. We will look at how to get email up and running on the iPhone.

Setting Up Email

The iPhone handles email well, and works with MobileMe and Microsoft Exchange. It handles pop3, IMAP and can work with Yahoo! Mail, Google Mail and AOL.

Setting up an email account

Don't forget

The iPhone can handle many types of email account. IMAP accounts are useful since you can see all your folders on the server, and can easily save email to specific folders.

Go to **Settings** > **General** > **Mail, Contacts, Calendars**

Enter your details including login **name** and **password**

Tap **Add Account** — make your choice from the options shown. You may need to use the **Other** option

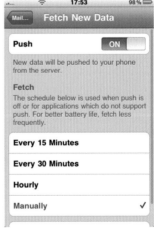

Decide how often you want your email delivered (**Every 15 minutes** uses more power than **Manually**)

You will need to set up the Push frequency, security settings and other features to make your email work correctly.

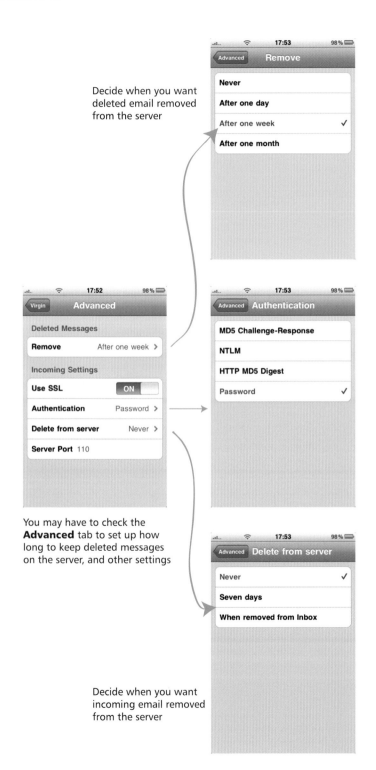

Decide when you want deleted email removed from the server

You may have to check the **Advanced** tab to set up how long to keep deleted messages on the server, and other settings

Decide when you want incoming email removed from the server

Beware

If you want to see your messages on the iPhone and your computer, make sure Delete from server is set to "Never".

Using Exchange Server

Mail can collect email, and sync calendars and contacts using Microsoft Exchange Server, which is great news for businesses.

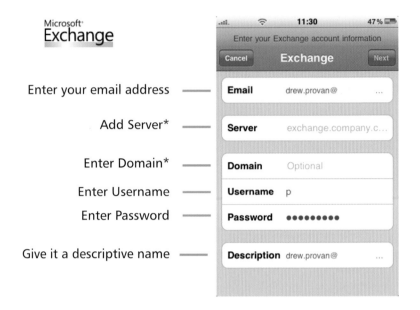

Enter your email address ——

Add Server* ——

Enter Domain* ——

Enter Username ——

Enter Password ——

Give it a descriptive name ——

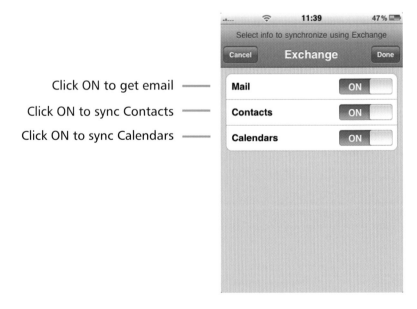

Click ON to get email ——

Click ON to sync Contacts ——

Click ON to sync Calendars ——

* You will need to ask your IT Administrator for these details

Email Viewing Settings

1 Go to **Settings** > **Mail, Contacts, Calendars**

2 Scroll down the list till you see **Mail**

3 **Adjust** settings for **Show**, **Preview**, **Minimum Font Size**, **Show To/Cc Label**, etc

Decide how many messages you wish to see, how many lines of preview, whether to **Show To/Cc Label**

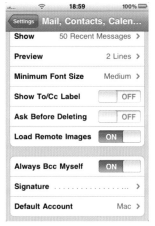

Do you want a copy of every email you send? If so, make sure **Always Bcc Myself** is **ON**

You can change the preview from **None** to **5 lines** of text

How large do you want the font?

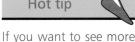

Hot tip

If you want to see more text on the screen set the font size to small.

Composing Email

1 Tap the **Mail** icon to open the app

2 Tap an **email account** to open it

3 Tap the **New Email** icon (bottom right). A new email will open

4 Tap the **To:** field and type the name of the recipient

5 Tap the **Subject:** and enter a subject for the email

6 Tap the **email body** area (below Subject:) and start typing your email

7 Insert a photo by selecting from Photos (touch and hold till you see **Copy** then touch and hold finger on email body till you see **Paste**. You can do the same with images in other apps, e.g., Safari

8 Once complete, hit **Send**

Hit send when done

Tap here and enter recipient name

Tap here and enter subject

Tap here to enter body of email

Reading Email

1   Check Mail icon for fresh mail — represented by a red circle. The number refers to the number of unread emails

2   Tap **Mail** to open

3   Tap the **Inbox** to open the email and if there is an attachment, you can tap to download

The red "1" above Mail shows you have one unread email. Tap Mail to open

Tap Inbox to open the email

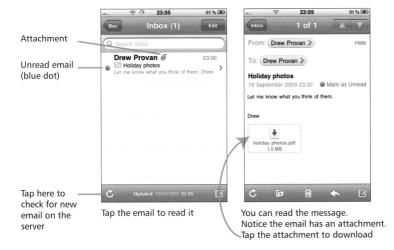

Attachment

Unread email (blue dot)

Tap here to check for new email on the server

Tap the email to read it

You can read the message. Notice the email has an attachment. Tap the attachment to download

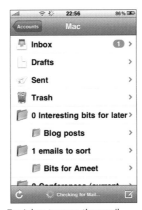

Hot tip

The paperclip icon shows you have received an attachment with an email.

...cont'd

Beware

Often, attachments do not download automatically. Tap the icon and you will see the attachment download. After downloading, tap to open.

Attachment is downloading

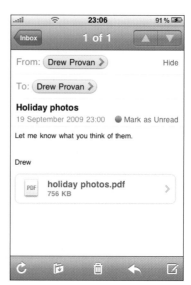

Tap to open

Hot tip

To save a photo from an email, touch and hold the photo till you see Save Image. Tap this, and the photo will be added to the Camera Roll.

Attachment opened

Forwarding Email

1   **Open** an email

2   Tap the **Reply/Forward** icon at the bottom right of the screen

3   Select **Forward**

4   **Enter the name of the recipient**

5   In the body of the email, enter any message you want to accompany the forwarded email

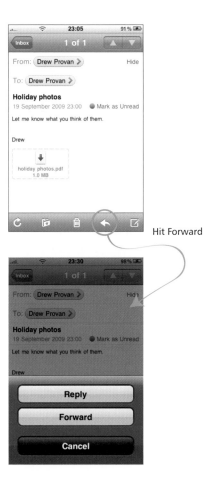

Hit Forward

Deleting Email

You can delete email a couple of different ways:

1 Tap the email to read it

2 When finished, tap the trash icon at the bottom of the screen

Alternative method

1 In the email list view slide your finger across the email (do not open it)

2 A red **Delete** box should appear

3 Tap delete and the email will be deleted

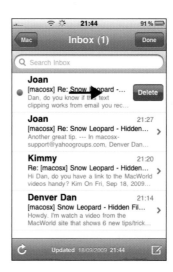

Yet another way of deleting email is:

1 Go to **Inbox** and tap the **Edit** button at the top right

2 Tap each email you want to delete and a red circle will appear in the left column

3 Hit **Delete** when you are ready to delete

Tap **Edit**

Tap the email you want to delete
A red circle with a check mark
will appear

Hit **Delete**

Move Email to Folders

If you have an IMAP account, such as a MobileMe account, you can see your folders on the server. You can move mail from your Inbox to another folder. This helps keep your mail organized, and your Inbox uncluttered.

Hot tip

Avoid having an Inbox full of read and new mail. Move items to folders (easy with IMAP accounts) or delete them.

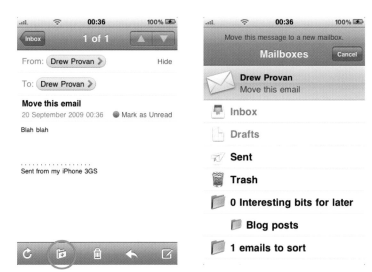

Tap the move icon and confirm you wish to move the email

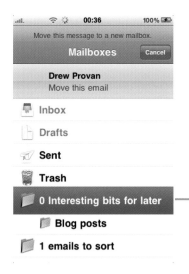

Tap the folder you wish to move it to and the email will jump into the folder

9 Accessibility Settings

The iPhone is well suited for people with visual problems. We will look at how to use Accessibility options on the iPhone.

Accessibility Settings

Many people with visual impairments should be able to make use of devices like the iPhone. With the standard default configuration they may run into problems, but the iPhone has many settings that can be modified to make them more usable.

What features are available?

- VoiceOver
- Zoom
- White on Black
- Mono Audio
- Speak Auto-text

Most of these features will work with most applications, apart from VoiceOver which will only work with the iPhone's standard (pre-installed) applications.

Switch on Accessibility

1. Plug the iPhone into your computer and make sure iTunes opens

2. Go to the **Summary** pane, check **Universal Access** in the options section

3. Within Universal Access, decide which features you want to activate

Alternative method

1. On the iPhone go to **Settings** > **General** > **Accessibility**

2. Scroll down the list of options and toggle on or off, depending on your needs

3. Switch each on or off using the iPhone or iTunes **Summary** pane

Switch on Universal Access in iTunes

Choose your options

Activate Settings on iPhone

Switching on VoiceOver

1   Go to **Settings** > **General** > **Accessibility**

2   Activate **VoiceOver** as shown below

3   When finished, you may wish to switch it off again

Switch on VoiceOver

Switch on Zoom to enlarge (Zoom and VoiceOver cannot be used together)

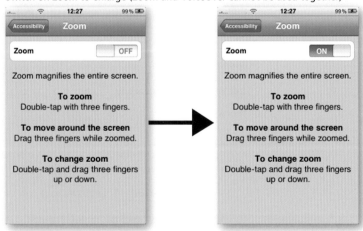

Other accessibility settings

1 Go to **Settings** > **General** > **Accessibility**

2 Activate **White on Black**

3 Activate **Zoom**

Beware

These settings are only found on the iPhone 3GS and 4G.

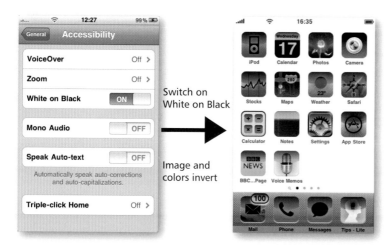

Switch on White on Black

Image and colors invert

Speak Auto-text ON

Actions on triple click Home Button

185

Thanks to Jonathan Bonnick of intelligentpublishing.com for the picture of the White on Black reversed image.

VoiceOver

Beware

These settings are only found on the iPhone 3GS and 4G.

VoiceOver

This speaks what's on the screen, so you can tell what's on the screen even if you cannot see it. It describes items on the screen and, if text is selected, VoiceOver will read the text.

Speaking rate

This can be adjusted using the settings.

Typing feedback

VoiceOver can provide this: go to **Settings** > **General** > **Accessibility** > **VoiceOver** > **Typing Feedback**.

Languages

VoiceOver is available in languages other than English (but is not available in all languages).

VoiceOver Gestures

When VoiceOver is active, the standard touchscreen gestures operate differently:

Tap	Speak item
Flick right or left	Select next or previous item
Flick up or down	Depends on Rotor Control setting
Two-finger tap	Stop speaking current item
Two-finger flick up	Read all from top of screen
Two-finger flick down	Read all from current position
Three-finger flick up or down	Scroll one page at a time
Three-finger flick right or left	Go to next or previous page
Three-finger tap	Speak the scroll status

Apple Support for VoiceOver

See: *http://support.apple.com/kb/HT3598.*

Zoom

The iPhone touchscreen lets you zoom in and out of elements on the screen. Zoom will let you magnify the whole screen, irrespective of which application you are running.

Turn Zoom on and off

1 Go to **Settings** > **General** > **Accessibility** > **Zoom**

2 Tap the Zoom **OFF/ON** switch

3 You cannot use Zoom and VoiceOver at the same time

Zoom in and out

1 **Double tap** the screen with three fingers

2 The screen will then magnify by 200%

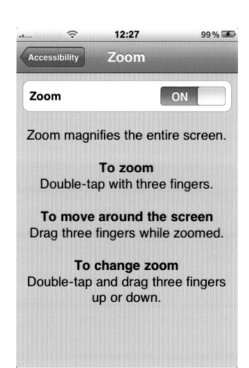

Increase magnification

1 Use **three fingers** and drag to the top of the screen (increase magnification) or bottom (decrease magnification).

2 Move around the screen

3 Drag or flick the screen with three fingers

Other Accessibility Settings

Beware

These settings are only found on the iPhone 3GS and 4G.

White on Black

This feature inverts the colors on the iPhone, which may make it easier for some people to read.

Activate White on Black

1 Go to **Settings** > **General** > **Accessibility**

2 Tap the **White on Black** switch

3 The screen should look like a photographic negative

Mono Audio

This combines the sound of both left and right channels into a mono audio signal played through both sides.

Turn Mono Audio on and off

1 Go to **Settings** > **General** > **Accessibility**

2 Switch on **Mono Audio**

Speak Auto-text

This setting enables the iPhone to speak text corrections and suggestions as you type text into the iPhone.

Turn Speak Auto-text on

① Go to **Settings** > **General** > **Accessibility**

② Switch on **Speak Auto-text**

③ Speak Auto-text works with VoiceOver and Zoom

Closed Captioning

This needs to be turned on in the iPod settings:

① Go to **Settings** > **iPod**

② Slide **Closed Captioning** button to **ON** to activate

Large phone keypad

The keypad of the iPhone is large, making it easy for people who are visually impaired to see the digits.

① Tap the **Phone** icon (on the dock)

② Tap the **keypad** icon (4th icon from left)

These settings are only found on the iPhone 3GS and 4G.

Apple Accessibility Support

The Apple Support area is great for all Apple products, and is especially helpful for iPhone Accessibility.

Check out the FAQs and watch the videos showing you how to set the iPhone up.

Log in to Apple support

Don't forget

Apple's website has masses of information about Accessibility.

1 Go to *http://www.apple.com/support/iphone*

2 Click on the Support pane

10 Working with Apps

There are thousands of apps for the iPhone, catering for every conceivable need. Here we will look at how to find apps, install them, and remove them. The chapter takes you through some of the apps in each category, to give you some idea of the range of programs available for the iPhone, both paid and free.

Installing Applications

Installing applications (apps) on the iPhone is incredibly easy, when you compare it to the cumbersome process used for installing programs onto a standard PDA. It's as simple as browsing the apps, choosing the one you want and tapping Install.

How many apps are there?

The app store was launched in January 2008, as an update to iTunes. By February 2009, there were 20,000 apps for download, and by October 2010 there were more than 300,000! In terms of downloads, Apple announced that by January 2009, 500 million apps had been downloaded, and by April 2009, they had reached the 1 billion mark!

Don't forget

You can browse apps on your iPhone or in iTunes. Installation can also be carried out using the computer or iPhone.

The App Store on your iPhone

1 On your iPhone tap **App Store**

2 Browse the apps by **Category, Featured, Top 25**

3 Or search for an app using the search function

Browse the App Store on your computer

1 Launch **iTunes**

2 Click the **App Store** pane

3 Find the app you want, click install

4 You will need to **enter your iTunes password**

5 The app will be downloaded and placed in the apps folder in iTunes

6 Next time you sync the iPhone the app will be copied across to the iPhone

The App Store on iTunes

This is shown below

1 Launch **iTunes** and select iTunes Store

2 Click the **App Store** tab and look for the **Categories** drop down menu

3 Select the category you are interested in, browse and download

Open iTunes and look for the AppStore pane

Browse the apps in iTunes

...cont'd

Browsing apps using the iPhone

1 Tap the App Store icon

2 Use the buttons on the bottom to view the apps

Featured apps   Categories   Top 25 apps   Search apps   3 apps have updates

Let Genius do the hard work

Once you have installed a few apps, Genius can help you choose further apps. This works in much the same way as Genius on iTunes, where it will suggest audio that fits well together. iTunes music Genius will create playlists for you. If you don't like the playlist you just ask Genius to suggest another playlist.

Here's what Genius suggests for me based on my previous downloads

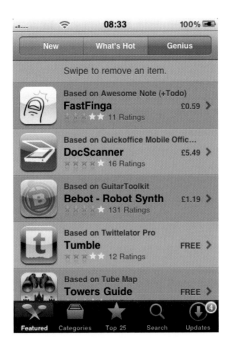

There are many ways to view the apps in the App Store:

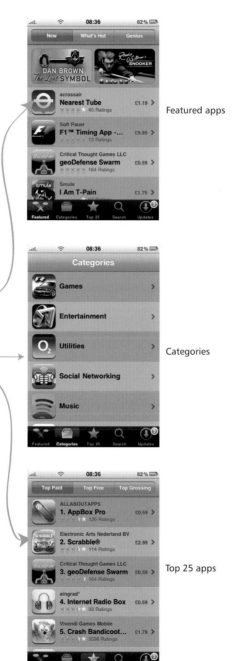

Featured apps

Categories

Top 25 apps

Tap the App Store icon to open and browse the apps using the tabs at the bottom of the screen

If you cannot find what you want try Searching for it

There are now so many apps, it may be difficult to find what you want. Try using the search tool and enter a word or words that describe what you are looking for.

195

Installation Process

1 Find the app you want using App Store on the iPhone

2 Tap the **Price** or **Free** tab

3 Tap **Install**

4 **Enter your iTunes password**

5 The app will install

Find app you want ("Boxed In")

Tap "Free"

Tap "Install"

Enter your iTunes password

Updating Apps

The publishers of apps provide updates which bring new features and improvements. You don't have to check your apps to see if there are updates — the App Store app itself will notify you by displaying a red circle with a number in it.

To update

1 Tap **App Store** and go to **Updates**

2 Tap the app shown — if multiple, tap **Update All**

3 **Enter password**, and the app(s) will update

Hot tip

If your App Store icon has a red circle with a number inside, it means there's an update for one or more of your apps. Keep them up-to-date since updated versions provide bug fixes and improvements.

197

Tap the app to update then tap "Free"

Enter your iTunes password

You can see the app downloading and then installing

Removing Apps

There are 2 ways to remove apps.

Using the iPhone

1 **Press and hold** the app you want to remove

2 All the apps on the screen will start jiggling and you will see an **x** at the top of the app

3 **Tap the x** and the app will be deleted

4 **Confirm** your action

5 Leave **feedback** if you wish

Tap the app but keep your finger on the icon — all the icons start to jiggle. Press the "x" on the app you wish to delete

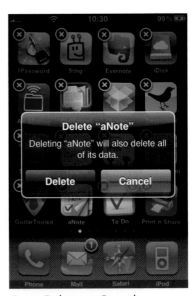

Press Delete or Cancel

Deleting apps using iTunes on your computer

1 Plug your iPhone into your PC or Mac

2 Make sure iTunes opens

3 Click the **iPhone tab** (in left pane)

4 Go to the **Applications** pane

5 Delete by **pressing** the **x** when you hover over the app's icon in the right window, or deactivate the app by unchecking its box in the left window

6 If you deactivate, but not delete permanently, you can put the app back on the iPhone by checking the box

7 The app will be restored to the iPhone next time you sync

Applications pane

Uncheck to remove it from the iPhone when you next sync (but the app is not deleted from your iTunes)

To permanently delete the app, hover over the icon with your mouse pointer and click the "x"

Apps Categories

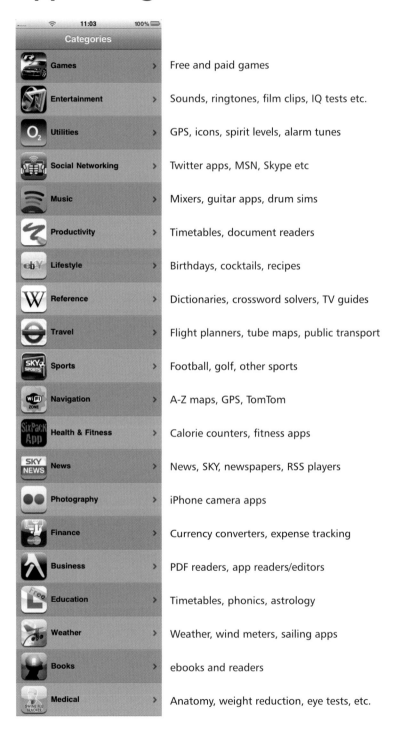

Games	Free and paid games
Entertainment	Sounds, ringtones, film clips, IQ tests etc.
Utilities	GPS, icons, spirit levels, alarm tunes
Social Networking	Twitter apps, MSN, Skype etc
Music	Mixers, guitar apps, drum sims
Productivity	Timetables, document readers
Lifestyle	Birthdays, cocktails, recipes
Reference	Dictionaries, crossword solvers, TV guides
Travel	Flight planners, tube maps, public transport
Sports	Football, golf, other sports
Navigation	A-Z maps, GPS, TomTom
Health & Fitness	Calorie counters, fitness apps
News	News, SKY, newspapers, RSS players
Photography	iPhone camera apps
Finance	Currency converters, expense tracking
Business	PDF readers, app readers/editors
Education	Timetables, phonics, astrology
Weather	Weather, wind meters, sailing apps
Books	ebooks and readers
Medical	Anatomy, weight reduction, eye tests, etc.

Games

App Store › Games › Clickgamer.com

Angry Birds

Game Center

Description

The survival of the Angry Birds is at stake. Dish out revenge on the green pigs who stole the Birds' eggs. Use the unique destructive powers of the Angry Birds to lay waste to the pigs' fortified castles. Angry Birds features hours of gameplay, challenging physics-based castle demolition, and lots of replay value. Each of the 195 levels requires logic, skill, and brute…

...More

Clickgamer.com Web Site ›   Angry Birds Support ›

App Store › Games › Simogo

Kosmo Spin

Description

Throughout the cosmos a distress call is heard...
"HELP US! FOR SOME REASON A FLYING SAUCER IS TRYING TO STEAL OUR BREAKFAST."
...

Simogo Web Site ›   Kosmo Spin Support ›

App Store › Games › Small Wonders

World of Popus

Game Center

Description

WORLD OF POPUS
...

...More

Small Wonders Web Site ›   World of Popus Support ›

App Store › Games › Firemint Pty Ltd

Real Racing

Game Center

Description

Coming soon ONLINE MULTIPLAYER via Game Center (free update)
...

...More

Firemint Pty Ltd Web Site ›   Real Racing Support ›

App Store › Games › Pinger, Inc.

StickWars 2 – Sequel to #1 Castle Defense Game

Description

Warning: Many stick figures were brutally harmed during the making of this game.
...

...More

Pinger, Inc. Web Site ›   StickWars 2 – Sequel to #1 Castle Defense Game Support ›

App Store › Games › 2DRockers

Into The Blue SD

Description

Into The Blue (SD) is a fun multi touch game where you need to protect your base against enemy spaceships. Keep your transporters under control and harvest crystals to survive.
...

...More

Into The Blue SD Support ›

App Store › Games › blacksmith games

Floop

Game Center

Description

PRESS QUOTES:
...

...More

Floop Support ›

Entertainment

App Store > Entertainment > Neave Interactive

Strobe Illusion

Description

Stare into the Strobe Illusion and begin to hallucinate!

After watching for 30 seconds your vision will distort and things around you will appear to move as if you're underwater or...

...More

Neave Interactive Web Site >   **Strobe Illusion Support >**

If you stare at the illusions long enough it distorts your vision. These illusions have been around for years in book form but this app brings these all together in one little handy package.

App Store > Entertainment > Damibu Ltd

DrivingFX Pro

Description

Do you remember your childhood days making driving noises as you played with your toy car? Were you the race car driver, skidding the wheels round the corners? Now, as you sit in your family car, do you still make the same noises? If so this Ap...

...More

DrivingFX Pro Support >

Now you can generate car noises while you are in the car, presumably better noises than your car actually makes.

App Store > Entertainment > Andela ICT

Magic6 (mentalism trick)

Description

Do you want to surprise your audience with a great mentalism act? Then you need this app.
Someone from the audience thinks of a number between 1 and 60. You can guess that with this App. They will be amazed.
...

...More

Andela ICT Web Site >   **Magic6 (mentalism trick) Support >**

A mentalism app where someone thinks of a number, and through sheer magic, this app tells you what that number was.

App Store > Entertainment > acrossair

Gyroscope

Description

An amazing visual gyroscope for your iPhone 4. This application displays a 3d gyroscope that acts just like a real gyroscope would and looks so real you'll want to touch it. And it acts as an educational tool too — flip main display over and learn about the maths and the history behind gyroscopes....

...More

acrossair Web Site >   **Gyroscope Support >**

This is an educational app since it emulates 3-D gyroscopes and is very realistic.

Utilities

App Store › Utilities › myNewApps.com

Battery Magic

Description

ALERT - The paid version, 'Battery Magic Elite' now has 1% Accuracy and is ON SALE for 99¢ for 2 days!!!

...

...More

myNewApps.com Web Site ›   **Battery Magic Support ›**

Battery utilities are big business, and there are loads of them on the App Store. This one makes a nice sound when you have reached full charge and has a large battery display.

App Store › Utilities › Hurryforward Ltd

DIY List

Description

DIY List is a handy list maker for Do-it-yourself enthusiasts, builders, decorators and interior designers.

Quickly add or delete items from the list. Create your own categories. Email your lists to a friend....

...More

Hurryforward Ltd Web Site ›   **DIY List Support ›**

Builders, home DIY enthusiasts, interior decorators and others should find this list-makes and to-do app useful.

App Store › Utilities › Andrea Ottolina

iTorch4 - iPhone4 Led Flashlight

Description

With iTorch4 for iPhone 4 you can:
✔ find your keys lost under the car;
✔ see the keyhole of your house door when back from a night out with friends;...

...More

iTorch4 - iPhone4 Led Flashlight Support ›

This app turns your iPhone into a torch which switches on very quickly. Useful when going upstairs in the dark, or if you lose your keys under the car.

App Store › Utilities › Code Drop

Safe Note

Description

☆ Currently #6 in 'What's Hot' ☆

...

...More

Code Drop Web Site ›   **Safe Note Support ›**

This app lets you keep notes, lists and reminders, away from prying eyes, by letting you password protect them.

Social Networking

App Store ▸ Social Networking ▸ TweetDeck

TweetDeck for iPhone

Description

TweetDeck is your mobile browser for staying in touch with what's happening now on Twitter from your iPhone or iPod Touch. TweetDeck shows you everything you want to see at once, so you can stay organised and up to date no matter where you are. ...

...More

TweetDeck Web Site ▸   TweetDeck for iPhone Support ▸

TweetDeck is very popular on the Mac and PC. It is a great-looking Twitter feed app which makes it easy to send tweets from your iPhone.

App Store ▸ Social Networking ▸ FTW Innovations

TextPics - Creative SMS Art for iPhone Texting

Description

☆ ☆ FEATURED APP ☆ ☆
☆ Top 10 in AppStores worldwide! ☆...

...More

FTW Innovations Web Site ▸   TextPics - Creative SMS Art for iPhone Texting Support ▸

Not exactly indispensable, but a fun way to add pics to messages — create the pics out of standard keyboard characters.

App Store ▸ Social Networking ▸ Skype Software S.a.r.l

Skype

Description

With Skype on your iPhone, iPod touch or iPad, you can make and receive calls, and instant message anyone else on Skype, wherever they are in the world. You can also save on international calls and text messages to phones. Skype is free to download and easy to use. With the latest version, you can now call over 3G*, and keep Skype running in the background....

...More

Skype Software S.a.r.l Web Site ▸   Skype Support ▸   Application Licence Agreement ▸

The ubiquitous Skype has now found a home on the iPhone with this great Skype app.

App Store ▸ Social Networking ▸ WhatsApp Inc.

WhatsApp Messenger

Description

WhatsApp messenger is a cross platform smartphone messenger currently available for iPhone, Android, BlackBerry and Nokia phones. The application utilizes push notifications to instantly get messages from friends, colleagues and family....

...More

WhatsApp Inc. Web Site ▸   WhatsApp Messenger Support ▸   Application Licence Agreement ▸

This is a cross-platform smartphone messenger (iPhone, Android, BlackBerry and Nokia) which lets you message your friends and receive push notifications.

Music

App Store › Music › Ultimate Guitar USA, LLC

Ultimate Guitar Tabs

Description

Ultimate Guitar Tabs is an easy and convenient application for viewing guitar Tablatures, bass Tablatures, drum Tablatures and chords. This is the only mobile application giving you UNLIMITED access to the world's largest database of Tabs from...

...More

Ultimate Guitar USA, LLC Web Site ›   Ultimate Guitar Tabs Support ›

If you can't quite work out what guitar chords are being played in your favorite music, this app will find the tablature for you and put you out of your misery.

App Store › Music › WM Company LLC

Piano Chord Key

Description

Play the chords of the key or create your own key. The Piano Chord Key app makes learning chords simple! Play the chord simply by tapping the row of the chord you would like to hear. You can browse and play chords by key, type of chord, or create your own key and chord progressions from the create tab of the app. Put together some of your favorite chords and...

...More

WM Company LLC Web Site ›   Piano Chord Key Support ›

As the title suggests, this app shows you what piano keys to hit when you want to generate chords. It helps with chord progressions, too.

App Store › Music › BLACKOUT LABS

Ringtone Designer Pro - Create Unlimited Ringtones

Description

☆ Now 50% off!!!!

-------------------------------...

...More

BLACKOUT LABS Web Site ›   Ringtone Designer Pro - Create Unlimited Ringtones Support ›

If you feel your iPhone has an insufficient number of ringtones, this app will let you generate a zillion more.

App Store › Music › Synsion Radio Technologies

TuneIn Radio

Description

Listen to and record over 40,000 radio stations including thousands of AM/FM local stations on your iPhone, iPod touch or iPad with TuneIn Radio!...

...More

Synsion Radio Technologies Web Site ›   TuneIn Radio Support ›

With this app you can listen to, and record, more than 40,000 AM/FM radiostations.

Productivity

This is an amazing piece of software for the Mac and PC and now it's available on the iPhone. Because of the iPhone's small screen it is trickier to use than the computer equivalents.

Now you can access your Dropbox files directly from your iPhone. If you don't have this for your computer — get it now!

With more than 300,000 apps for the iPhone it is becoming very difficult to find what you're looking for. Why not get an app that helps you find apps?

App Store ▸ Productivity ▸ Good.iWare Ltd.

GoodReader for iPhone

Description

Quick summary: super-robust PDF reader with advanced reading, annotating, markup and highlighting capabilities, excellent file manager, TXT file reader and editor, audio/video player, Safari-like viewer for MS Office and iWorks files.
------------...

...More

Good.iWare Ltd. Web Site ▸   GoodReader for iPhone Support ▸

This is one of the available PDF readers for the iPhone. Does a nice job, and has a clear interface.

Lifestyle

eBay Mobile

Description

The eBay application for the iPhone is specially designed to run natively on the Apple iPhone and the iPod Touch. Using a streamlined interface that's as elegant as it is practical, eBay members can search, bid, and check their activity on the go. Buyers can sneak in that last-minute bid on a hard-to-find item, sellers can check on their sales, and act on time-sensitive...
...More

eBay Inc. Web Site ›   eBay Mobile Support ›   Application Licence Agreement ›

Most of us use eBay but using a browser to check your auctions on the iPhone is not great. This app solves all those problems.

AroundMe

Description

AroundMe allows you to quickly find out information about your surroundings.

How many times have you found yourself in need of finding the closest Gas Station?...
...More

Tweakersoft Web Site ›   AroundMe Support ›

You can find out about local banks, coffee houses, gas stations and much more with this clever app.

Jamie's 20 Minute Meals

Description

Hi Guys,
...
...More

Zolmo Web Site ›   Jamie's 20 Minute Meals Support ›

Jamie Oliver seems to be everywhere so why not on the iPhone. The app has loads of his best recipes and cooking tips.

London's Best Coffee

Description

Download to discover over 50 of the best independent cafes and stalls serving locally roasted coffee in London. The app is not only a useful tool for finding the best coffee near you, but it also informs you of the type of beans and machines each cafe uses....
...More

blue crow media Web Site ›   London's Best Coffee Support ›

This app will point you in the direction of the best places in London to have coffee. The title says it all.

Reference

An encyclopedic app containing loads of useful tidbits about the world.

If you can't solve this incredibly popular iPhone game by fair means you can cheat using this app. In case you've missed it, this app is the most popular game at the moment.

This app pulls together all the Google applications into one neat app but it does take you to a browser to use the actual applications themselves. Still very useful.

This has definitions of more than 200,000 words. It also has an advanced spellchecker and a thesaurus.

Travel

London Tube Deluxe

Description

"A must for Londoners." - London Evening Standard. London Tube Deluxe is the Most full featured & No. 1 selling guide to the London Underground.....

...More

Malcolm Barclay Web Site >   **London Tube Deluxe Support >**

There are several Tube map apps out there but this one does it even better. It has journey planner, departure boards, and is multilingual.

Google Earth

Description

Hold the world in the palm of your hand. With Google Earth for iPhone, iPad, and iPod touch, you can fly to far corners of the planet with just the swipe of a finger. Explore the same global satellite and aerial imagery available in the desktop version of Google Earth, including high-resolution imagery for over half of the world's population and a third of the world's land mass. ...

...More

Google Web Site >   **Google Earth Support >**   **Application Licence Agreement >**

This remains an amazing application on the computer and the iPhone version is superb too.

New York Guide - mTrip

Description

The most intelligent travel guide! Extensive directory of places to visit, customizable & automated trip itineraries, off-line maps & navigation, augmented reality and trip sharing. ★ "Don't travel without them." iPhone Life"★ Watch the DEMO at...

...More

mTrip Travel Guides Web Site >   **New York Guide - mTrip Support >**

This NY guide tells you about attractions, museums, landmarks, restaurants, bars, hotels, and a whole lot more.

TravelJabs

Description

Travel Jabs brought to you by AllClear Travel provides you with vaccination information by country.

AllClear Insurance Services Web Site >   **TravelJabs Support >**

What's New In Version 1.2

Going abroad can be confusing in terms of what vaccines to have and this very useful app will advise travelers before they set off as to which vaccines they need to have before they go.

Sports

You can listen to talkSPORT on your iPhone using this app.
There is live streaming and live slideshows. You can also share
the sports news using social networks.

Provides live scores for UK, European and International
football teams.

Live video content and interviews. However, to use the app you
will need a Sky Mobile TV subscription.

App Store › Sports › NBA

NBA Game Time

Description

NBA Game Time 2010 is the official App of the NBA. Featuring a Weekly Live Game, Daily Video Highlights, Games on Demand, Home and Away Radio Broadcasts, Real Time Stats and Scores, News, Photos, and more. Purchase League Pass from within the app to watch every NBA Game, or authenticate your Premium online League Pass subscription. With over 5…

...More

NBA Web Site ›   NBA Game Time Support ›   Application Licence Agreement ›

This is the official app of the NBA. It displays video highlights
of games, and provides Games on Demand.

Navigation

App Store › Navigation › TomTom International BV

TomTom U.K. & Ireland

Description

Get the TomTom navigation app and have smart, easy-to-use, turn-by-turn navigation on your iPhone or iPod touch, whenever and wherever you need it....

...More

TomTom International BV Web Site ›   TomTom U.K. & Ireland Support ›

Now the industry-standard in GPS navigation devices, TomTom has made it to the iPhone. Very useful for those of us who are geographically-challenged.

App Store › Navigation › pinkfroot limited

Plane Finder

Description

✈The original and most highly rated plane tracking app, ranked number one in the Navigation category in over 20 countries.✈ ...

...More

pinkfroot limited Web Site ›   Plane Finder Support ›

You can track flights using this app if you know the flight number you want to track.

App Store › Navigation › Tyler Bell

L.E.D. Torch

Description

#1 Sold LED Torch App in the App Store. Sold 40000 Copies In 130 COUNTRIES.
...

...More

L.E.D. Torch Support ›   Application Licence Agreement ›

Another app which makes your iPhone light up like a torch. Helpful when you're in a dark place and have forgotten to bring a torch with you.

App Store › Navigation › Ombros Brands Inc.

ATM Locator - Find the Nearest ATMs

Description

Find the nearest ATM (Automated Teller Machine) just about anywhere in the world! ATM Locator keeps track of the more then 1 million cash machines around the globe. You can now find cash and other services 24 hours a day, seven days a week....

...More

Ombros Brands Inc. Web Site ›   ATM Locator - Find the Nearest ATMs Support ›

Rather than wander for miles looking for a hole in the wall, this app will tell you where the nearest ATM is located.

Health & Fitness

App Store > Health & Fitness > Alistair Ewing

iRipped

Description

Imagine having your own personal bodybuilder/dietitian/resistance training expert in your own pocket, now you can with iRipped.

...

...More

iRipped Support >

The ultimate app for getting the ripped look you always dreamed of. Provides great photos of the exercises, diet and sleep advice and a load more.

App Store > Health & Fitness > Medical Productions

iFitness

Description

LIMITED TIME SALE Raved about by The New York Times, Washington Post, ABC News and the countless people that have made iFitness the #1 selling fitness app worldwide! Achieve your goal of getting and staying fit with iFitness. iFitness...

...More

Medical Productions Web Site >   iFitness Support >

Another work-out app for those seeking the body-beautiful. Useful information in terms of workouts aimed at all levels from beginner to the seasoned pro.

App Store > Health & Fitness > Weight Watchers International, Inc.

Weight Watchers Mobile UK

Description

It's more convenient than ever to connect to Weight Watchers from wherever you are. EVERYONE who downloads our App can: ...

...More

Weight Watchers International, Inc. Web Site >   Weight Watchers Mobile UK Support >
Application Licence Agreement >

For those wishing to lose weight, the people at Weight Watchers have put together this handy app that tells you what to eat and tracks your progress.

App Store > Health & Fitness > Chello Publishing

Carbs & Cals - A visual guide to Carbohydrate & Calorie Counting

Description

This is the Carbohydrate and Calorie Counting App you have always wanted! It contains over 1200 food photographs so you can more easily judge the carbs and calories in your food and drinks than ever before!...

...More

Chello Publishing Web Site >   Carbs & Cals - A visual guide to Carbohydrate & Calorie Counting Support >

This app helps you work out what to eat and what not to eat.

News

World-acclaimed BBC news have put this app together so you can keep on top of current news on your iPhone.

Get the Economist news stories on your iPhone. Provides the Editor's selection and must-read articles.

Cool app for saving long web pages and blogs so you can read them offline later. There are numerous user settings such as fonts, size, and others to help make the content more readable for you.

This is a satirical app which brings together current events and gossip in one fun app.

Photography

App Store ▸ Photography ▸ Adobe Systems Incorporated

Adobe Photoshop Express

Description

ADOBE® PHOTOSHOP® EXPRESS: Edit and share — anywhere

...

...More

Adobe Systems Incorporated Web Site ▸   Adobe Photoshop Express Support ▸
Application Licence Agreement ▸

Photoshop is a great program for tidying up and creating special effects on your photos on the Mac or PC and now it's available on the iPhone.

App Store ▸ Utilities ▸ CocoaTek

Camera One : ALL-IN-1

Description

The FIRST app which supports GeoTag in iPhone photo album!
The best ALL-IN-1 iPhone Camera App! (For iPhone or iPod touch 4 Only)...

...More

CocoaTek Web Site ▸   Camera One : ALL-IN-1 Support ▸

There are loads of camera apps for the iPhone but this one seems to be several apps in one, providing color effects, zoom, antishake, geotagging and time-stamping. Very useful.

App Store ▸ Photography ▸ Lucky Clan

ArtStudio - draw, paint and edit photo

Description

25% off the regular price for a limited time! BUY NOW AND GET FREE UPDATES FOREVER!

...

...More

Lucky Clan Web Site ▸   ArtStudio - draw, paint and edit photo Support ▸

Add effects to your photos using this painting and drawing app. There are tons of brushes and effects available to play with.

App Store ▸ Photography ▸ Apple Inc.

iMovie

iMovie.
Make beautiful HD movies anywhere.

iMovie on the Mac makes movie editing easy and the same is true of Apple's iPhone version.

Finance

Account Tracker

Description

An easy to use account tracking, budgeting and expense management application that helps you keep track of your money.
...

...More

Graham Haley Web Site ›   **Account Tracker Support ›**

This app is great for account tracking, budgeting, managing your expenses and even has bill reminders.

iBank

Description

iBank Mobile lets you track your day-to-day spending and monitor account balances on the go. It's easy to enter and categorize transactions, track expenses, or view running balances — all from your iPhone or iPod touch....

...More

IGG Software, LLC Web Site ›   **iBank Support ›**

With this app you can track day to day spending, monitor your accounts, check your balances and track expenses.

PayPal

Description

Send money to your friends, manage your account, and more, with the PayPal app. It's free, secure and more convenient than going to the ATM, writing checks, or sending gifts the traditional way.
• Send money as gifts, collect money for a group gift, or repay a friend for FREE*...

...More

PayPal, an eBay Company Web Site ›   **PayPal Support ›**

PayPal is the preferred method of payment for eBay and many websites now and it's great to have PayPal as a separate app on the iPhone.

MoneyBook

Description

It may look simplistic, but MoneyBook is a powerful personal finance app that offers unique features in a beautiful, easy-to-use user interface. There's even an amazing free companion web app with it....

...More

noidentity Web Site ›   **MoneyBook Support ›**

Great for personal finance, and has a companion web app. You can export your transactions as emails and the app will help you with your budgeting.

Business

Documents To Go® Premium - Office Suite

Description

"WHAT'S NEW IN 4.0" Speed enhancements, external keyboard support, Sheet To Go freeze panes and sort, multi-tasking, high resolution retina display & more! ...

...More

DataViz, Inc. Web Site >   Documents To Go® Premium - Office Suite Support >

If you ever need to edit Microsoft Office files on the iPhone this app will make the task easy. You can sync files from your desktop to your iPhone once you download the mini DTG app for Mac or PC.

PDF Reader Pro

Description

Macworld review: PDF Reader Pro ran fast on an iPhone 3GS and never crashed. PDF files look perfect. I recommend it for the ease-of-use, file-upload system, and accurate rendering.★★ Limited time on Sale ! ★★...

...More

YUYAO Mobile Software, Inc. Web Site >   PDF Reader Pro Support >

Another PDF reader. Fully functional and does the job very nicely.

Dragon Dictation

Description

Dragon Dictation is an easy-to-use voice recognition application powered by Dragon® NaturallySpeaking® that allows you to easily speak and instantly see your text or email messages. In fact, it's up to five (5) times faster than typing on the keyboar...

...More

Nuance Communications Web Site >   Dragon Dictation Support >

Rather than type your emails and text why not dictate and let Dragon do the transcription? Easy to use.

Creative Whack Pack

Description

The Creative Whack Pack's 84 creativity strategies stimulate you to think creatively.
• "The most impressive brainstorming tool in the App Store, hands down." —Innovation Tools...

...More

Creative Think Web Site >   Creative Whack Pack Support >

If you are ever stuck for ideas and need to brainstorm this app is for you.

Education

Tiny Garden

Description

Tiny Garden is an educational game that helps children learn new words as they play. Tiny Garden delights and encourages children to explore words in an interactive musical garden that is full of animated animals, plants, fruit & vegetables. Childr...

...More

Milo Creative Web Site ›　　**Tiny Garden Support ›**

Helps children learn new words as they play. You can record your own words and several languages are available.

Maths Addicted

Description

"This app has been specialy elaborated for kids.
Teaching math have never been easier and fun.
...

...More

TakeItBeHappy Web Site ›　　**Maths Addicted Support ›**

This little app makes math a bit more interesting.

Design and Technology

Description

The Design and Technology application provides students with a new way to learn, work and prepare for tests and exams in many areas of Design and Technology. Study on the bus, in your home or in school without the need to carry your books. You can even listen to your music at the same time....

...More

J Plimmer Web Site ›　　**Design and Technology Support ›**

Now a regular school subject the D&T app helps kids get more out of their studies. The app includes quizzes and other features to help with learning in a fun way.

Star Walk - 5 stars astronomy guide

Description

Featured by Apple - Best Apps of 2009!
Enjoy enhanced stargazing experience with gyroscope on iPhone 4 and full iOS 4 support with multitasking!...

...More

Vito Technology Inc. Web Site ›　　**Star Walk - 5 stars astronomy guide Support ›**

This is your personal planetarium providing all you need to know about the cosmos, with a ton of features that make astronomy even more interesting.

Weather

App Store › Weather › International Travel Weather Calculator

Weather+

Description

Weather+ is setting a new standard for Weather applications!

...

...More

Weather+ Support ›

Provides weather information for a number of cities, full screen video loops of weather, wind direction and speed, world time and much more.

App Store › Weather › AccuWeather, Inc.

AccuWeather.com

Description

Get the "Best Weather on the Web" wherever you go with the AccuWeather.com GPS application for iPhone. This worldwide forecasting tool has all the free features you need to "weatherproof" your day.

...

...More

AccuWeather, Inc. Web Site ›   AccuWeather.com Support ›   Application Licence Agreement ›

This weather app provides 15-day forecasts, and provides severe weather information and forecast videos.

App Store › Weather › The Weather Channel Interactive

The Weather Channel®

Description

The Weather Channel takes your weather experience to the next level with full screen maps, extended forecasts, severe weather alerts, and more.

...

...More

The Weather Channel Interactive Web Site ›   The Weather Channel® Support ›

Uses Google Maps for fast zooming and panning. It pinpoints your location at launch and has Facebook integration.

App Store › Weather › Sotic Ltd

Ski Club Snow Reports

Description

The Ski Club of Great Britain snow report app, brought to you in association with Land Rover, provides you with the best and most respected snow reports from 250 ski resorts around the world, updated daily for the most current snow conditions.

...

...More

Sotic Ltd Web Site ›   Ski Club Snow Reports Support ›

Covers 250 ski resorts, snow depths, piste conditions, and live weather with web cams. For those who love to ski this has to be one app you can't live without.

Books

Apple's ebook app, as featured on the iPad is also on the iPhone. You can browse, buy, read and store ebooks and PDFs for reading anywhere you want. Tons of user settings to make the reading even easier.

App Store › Books › Amazon.com

Kindle

Description

The Kindle app is optimized for the iPad, iPhone, and iPod touch, giving users the ability to read Kindle books on a beautiful, easy-to-use interface. You'll have access to over 750,000* books in the Kindle Store, including best sellers and new releases. Amazon Whispersync automatically syncs your last page read, bookmarks, notes, and highlights across devices...

...More

Amazon.com Web Site ›   Kindle Support ›   Application Licence Agreement ›

This app is the gateway to Kindle books which you can buy and read just as you would with iBooks. There's a huge selection of books to choose from.

App Store › Books › Wattpad

100,000 Free Books - Wattpad

Description

Wattpad is the world's most popular ebook community. Also known as YouTube for ebooks, it's a place where where readers and writers discover, share and connect. With over 1 million downloads per month, Wattpad is the world's most widely used mobile ebook application and one of the world's largest collections of originally-created ebooks. Wattpad gives you FREE...

...More

Wattpad Web Site ›   100,000 Free Books - Wattpad Support ›

This app is for the popular ebook community which hosts a large collection of books for you to download and read.

App Store › Books › Marvel Entertainment

Marvel Comics

Description

Introducing the MARVEL COMICS app, a revolutionary new way to experience the Marvel Universe on your iPhone, iPod Touch and iPad, featuring the world's most popular super heroes! Download hundreds of comic books featuring your favorite characters -- including Iron Man, Thor, Captain America, Spider-Man, Wolverine and more -- on your mobile device with t...

...More

Marvel Entertainment Web Site ›   Marvel Comics Support ›

Features all your favorites such as Iron Man, Captain America and others. You can also back up your books using the website.

Medical

App Store › Medical › MedHand – Mobile Libraries

Oxford Handbook of Clinical Medicine, Eighth Edition

Description

As ubiquitous in hospitals as stethoscopes, the Oxford Handbook of Clinical Medicine is a guiding star for all medical students, junior doctors and trainees. The culmination of more than 20 years' clinical experience, and containing the...

...More

MedHand – Mobile Libraries Web Site ›   Oxford Handbook of Clinical Medicine, Eighth Edition Support ›
Application Licence Agreement ›

Very popular handbook with medical students and junior doctors worldwide, now available for the iPhone which means you get all the useful medical know-how without the bulk of carrying a physical book.

App Store › Medical › Handmark, Inc.

Medical - Oxford Dictionary

Description

Powered by Handmark, this market-leading illustrated dictionary contains 12,500 authoritative entries on all aspects of medical science. Written by a team of medical experts, all entries have been revised and updated for this new edition to reflect the very latest in medical knowledge and practice. Entries are accessible and jargon-free and are complemented by...

...More

Handmark, Inc. Web Site ›   Medical - Oxford Dictionary Support ›

World-famous medical dictionary now available for the iPhone. Very useful for doctors, their secretaries and anyone who needs access to medical terminology and spelling.

App Store › Medical › Agile Partners

The Merck Manual - Professional Edition

Description

"The Merck Manual has always been highly regarded for its clarity and focus on delivering just the right amount of information. This app for iPhone, iPod touch and iPad provides the information in a convenient form that will make it even more valuable for healthcare professionals on the go." - Robert S. Porter, MD, Editor-in-Chief...

...More

Agile Partners Web Site ›   The Merck Manual - Professional Edition Support ›

The Merck Manual is a compendium of symptoms, signs and diagnostic information. Popular for many years in book form.

App Store › Medical › FreeApps

Relax Waterfall

Description

Absolutely Relaxing!
Do feel stressed? Overworked? Not Satisfied with life? Wish you can relax? Want to Sleep Better?...

...More

FreeApps Web Site ›   Relax Waterfall Support ›

This little app helps you to de stress and it's free!

11 Solving Problems

*The iPhone occasionally misbehaves —
an app will not close, or the iPhone may
malfunction. This section looks at how to
fix common problems and provides some
helpful websites. The chapter also helps
you find your lost or stolen iPhone.*

General iPhone Care

The iPhone is a fairly robust gadget but, like any complex piece of electronic hardware, it may suffer from knocks, scratches, getting wet and other problems.

Cleaning the body and screen

The touchscreen is supposed to be scratch resistant. In fact, there are YouTube videos showing people trying to scratch the screen by placing the iPhone into a plastic bag containing keys and shaking the whole thing around. Amazingly, the screen seems not to scratch. Then they put it in a blender and it, well, got blended. So it's definitely not blender-proof!

Paper kitchen towel, wetted with a little water containing a couple of drops of washing up liquid, is great for getting rid of heavily greased screens.

The iPhone is supplied with a small glass cleaning cloth (it should be in the small black cardboard package shown above). The best way to clean is to make sure there is no grit or sand on the body or screen and gently rub with the cleaning cloth. This should bring back the shine without scratching the glass or the back of the phone.

Occasionally the screen may get very greasy and a little soap helps to get the grease off:

1. Put a few drops of washing-up liquid in warm water

2. Get some paper kitchen towel and dip this into the water

3. Make sure the kitchen towel is not dripping and lightly wipe over the screen and rest of the casing

4. Dry off using the black iPhone cleaning cloth

Keep iPhone Up-to-Date

Apple releases updates to the iPhone operating system periodically.

These are downloaded and installed using iTunes.

Is your iPhone fully up to date?

1 Plug your iPhone into **iTunes**

2 Click **Check for Update**

3 Follow any instructions

Don't forget

Software updates for iPhone users are provided free by Apple. If one becomes available, download and install it.

Click here to see if there are any updates

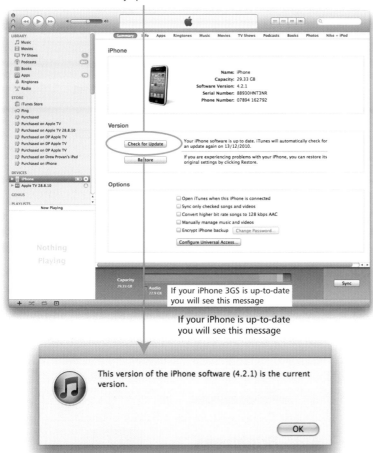

If your iPhone 3GS is up-to-date you will see this message

If your iPhone is up-to-date you will see this message

This version of the iPhone software (4.2.1) is the current version.

OK

Maximize iPhone Battery

The iPhone is a bit of a power hog. Browsing the web, listening to music and watching videos drains power. If you only make a few phone calls each day, your iPhone will last a couple of days between charges. But most people use it for far more than this and their battery will last about a day.

Tweaks to ensure maximum battery life

Hot tip

You can conserve battery power by switching off Wi-Fi and Bluetooth. Instead of opting for push email, you can check for email manually.

224

1 **Switch OFF Wi-Fi** if you don't need it

2 **Switch off Bluetooth** if you don't need it

3 Switch on battery percentage indicator

4 **Switch off 3G** if you don't need this

5 Collect your **email manually**

6 Set **Auto-lock** to a short period, e.g. 1 minute

7 Always hit the **OFF** button when you have finished using the iPhone (screen goes black which uses less power)

8 Reduce the **brightness** of your screen

9 Consider using **Airplane mode** for maximum conservation of power!

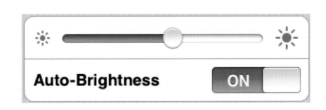

Restart, Force Quit and Reset

Restart the iPhone

If the iPhone misbehaves, or applications act strangely, you can restart the iPhone.

1 **Hold down** the Sleep/Wake button

2 When you see the **Slide to Power Off** appear, **push this to the right**

3 Leave the iPhone for a couple of minutes then press the **Sleep/Wake** button again and let the phone restart

Force Quit an app

Sometimes apps misbehave and you want to quit them and reopen. To do this, press the Home Button twice to bring up the app tray.

Touch and hold an app until they all jiggle and you see the quit icon next to each. Touch the quit icon to quit the app.

Touch and hold the apps, then touch ⊖ to quit an app

Reset the iPhone

1 Press the **Sleep/Wake** and the **Home Button** at the same time

2 The screen will suddenly turn black and the iPhone will restart

Apple Resources

Visit Apple!

The first place you should look for help is the Apple site. After all, iPhone is their creation so they should know more than anyone.

The iPhone and iPhone Support areas are packed with information, tutorials and videos.

Useful URLs

http://www.apple.com/iphone/

http://www.apple.com/support/iphone/

Technology Experts

David Pogue's Top 10 iPhone tips …

on the O'Reilly site are worth reading (David Pogue is always worth reading — he loves technology and loves all things Apple).

Useful URLs

http://broadcast.oreilly.com/2009/07/david-pogues-top-10-tips-for-t.html

David's New York Times blog is fantastic, and you can find it here *http://pogue.blogs.nytimes.com/*

Visit the iPhone Lounge!

There is an iPod lounge which has long provided loads of hints and tips for iPods. These guys review hardware, accessories and provide reviews of new gear for the iPod and the iPhone.

What does the site offer?

1 News

2 Reviews of apps and accessories

3 Forums

4 Software

5 Help

6 Articles

Other Useful websites

I Use This

Provides reviews of iPhone apps, and lets you know how many people are actually using the apps.

What's on iPhone

Largely a review site but it also provides information about hardware and for people interested in developing for the iPhone.

Restoring the iPhone

Sometimes things go wrong and your iPhone needs to be restored. This is similar to a PC which goes wrong — you can restore from a restore point. iTunes will make a backup of your iPhone each time you plug it in to sync.

To restore to a previous point:

1 **Plug the iPhone** into the PC or Mac, open iTunes and go to the Summary pane

2 Click **Restore** and follow the instructions

Click Restore to restore the iPhone to a previous restore point

You will see this message. Click Restore if you are sure you want to perform this action

If You Lose Your iPhone

Apple has built in a new feature to the iPhone, which allows you to erase the entire contents of your iPhone remotely. This means that if it gets stolen, you can remotely erase the iPhone and prevent whoever stole your iPhone from getting their hands on your personal data. At present this is only available for people who have signed up to MobileMe.

Set up Find My iPhone

1 **Log in to MobileMe** (*http://www.me.com*)

2 Go to the **Settings** options

3 Look for **Find My iPhone**

4 **Click the tab** and set up the various options

5 If you are really sure the iPhone has been stolen, activate **Remote Wipe** to prevent any private data being viewed by the thief

Hot tip

If for no other reason, it is worth getting a MobileMe account so you can track your iPhone and erase the contents if it gets stolen.

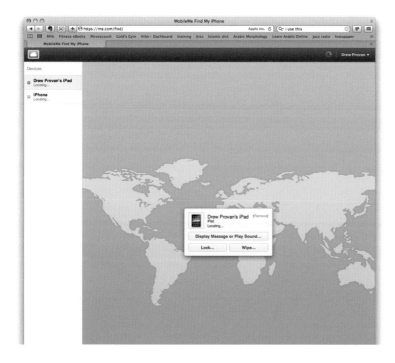

...cont'd

Locating your iPhone

Maybe you were out late and dropped your iPhone but can't quite remember where? Or perhaps it's in the house but you are not 100% sure. If you use MobileMe to look for the location of your iPhone it may help you recover the iPhone. Certainly, if it's at home you will soon know, because the map location will show you where the iPhone is. The iPhone does actually have to be on, and transmitting to the cellular network, in order for Find My iPhone to work.

1   **Log into MobileMe** and go to **Settings**

2   Click **Find My iPhone**

3   Check map location and recover the iPhone, if possible

Index

E

F

G

H

I